Seafood and Things from the Outer Banks

A Collection of Recipes by

Jerry G. Smith
Chef Dirt
Outer Banks • North Carolina

Printed in 2000
Cover and Recipes
Copyright © 1998
by Jerry G. Smith

Dividers and Cooking Hints
Copyright © 1998
Cookbooks by Morris Press
ISBN #0-9662656-0-2

Printed in the U.S.A. by

P.O. Box 2110 • Kearney, NE 68848

23179 j   1

Acknowledgements & Appreciation

"Seafood and Things" is now into the third printing. I would like to express my thanks and gratitude for the books success to my many friends whom, have and will select this book for reading and using.

I am truly honored that you have chosen it to be placed in your home.

A few of the recipes in this book were given to me by family members, their names and relationships are printed at the bottom of the recipe. My grandchildren didn't have one to submit so I gave them credit for one of mine, other than that all the recipes in this book belong to me. So if you don't like them there is no one else to blame. But all kidding aside, every recipe in this book is good or it wouldn't be in here. I know, for instance, that not everyone will like tuna, so I tried to include something everyone would like, I think I have.

Don't be afraid to substitute ingredients or customize to your own taste. Remember if you don't like it, how can you expect someone else to like it.

I cannot stress enough the importance of presentation, if a dish looks good you have achieved 50 percent success even before it's served. Use things like; spiral mushrooms, lemon and radish roses, citrus slices and curls, carrot and celery curls, etc., etc. Treat your dishes as you would a beautiful painting, you would not think of displaying it unframed.

If you have a problem or question about any of the recipes in this book, or if you want to cook something that is not addressed, or any other cooking question, call me at (252) 491-2403.

There are two kinds of cooks you never forget. Great ones and bad ones.

Now let's get started and live to eat, not eat to live.

Jerry G. Smith
Chef Dirt

Special Thanks

To My Wife "Becky Smith"
who has the enormous job of
marketing, designing, compiling
and distributing of all cookbooks.

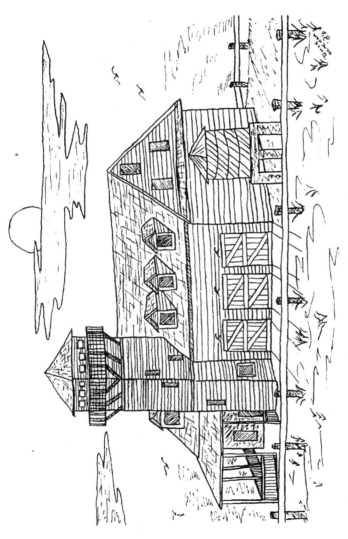

Hatteras Island Life Saving Station

Capt. Tommie Beacham is a local artist and 9th generation native of the Outer Banks.

Table of Contents

Appetizers

&

Beverages

Helpful Hints

- You won't need sugar with your tea if you drink jasmine tea or any of the lighter-bodied varieties, like Formosa Oolong, which have their own natural sweetness. They are fine for sugarless iced tea, too.

- Calorie-free club soda adds sparkle to iced fruit juices, makes them go further and reduces calories per portion.

- For tea flavoring, dissolve old-fashioned lemon drops or hard mint candy in your tea. They melt quickly and keep the tea brisk!

- Most diets call for 8 ounces of milk and 4 ounces of fruit juice. Check your glassware. Having the exact size glass ensures the correct serving amount.

- Make your own spiced tea or cider. Place orange peels, whole cloves, and cinnamon sticks in a 6-inch square piece of cheesecloth. Gather the corners and tie with a string. Steep in hot cider or tea for 10 minutes or longer if you want a stronger flavor.

- Always chill juices or sodas before adding to beverage recipes.

- To cool your punch, float an ice ring made from the punch rather than using ice cubes. Not only is this more decorative, but it also inhibits melting and diluting.

- Place fresh or dried mint in the bottom of a cup of hot chocolate for a cool and refreshing taste.

- One lemon yields about ¼ cup juice; one orange yields about ⅓ cup juice. This is helpful in making fresh orange juice or lemonade!

- Never boil coffee; it brings out the acid and causes a bitter taste. Store ground coffee in the refrigerator or freezer to keep it fresh.

- Always use COLD water for electric drip coffee makers. Use 1 to 2 tablespoons ground coffee for each cup of water.

- Seeds and nuts, both shelled and unshelled, keep best and longest when stored in the freezer. Unshelled nuts crack more easily when frozen. Nuts and seeds can be used directly from the freezer.

- Cheeses should be served at room temperature, approximately 70°.

Appetizers & Beverages

CRAB DIP

24 oz. cream cheese, softened
1 lb. back fin crabmeat (remove all shell)
1 T. fresh chopped parsley
1 T. finely chopped sweet onion
1 T. capers
1/3 c. mayonnaise

1/4 tsp. liquid smoke
1 tsp. Tabasco sauce
1 T. Texas Pete's hot sauce
1 tsp. Worcestershire sauce
1 T. Paul Prudhomme's Seafood Magic

Put capers, onion, parsley, liquid smoke, Texas Pete, Tabasco, Worcestershire sauce and Seafood Magic in food processor and process until almost liquid. Set mixture aside. Place crab in food processor and process for 5 seconds. Combine mayonnaise, cream cheese, processed sauce mixture and crab in a mixing bowl and mix on high speed until all ingredients are well blended. Makes about 3½ pounds and can be stored in refrigerator up to 7 days. **This is a crab lovers treat.**

SALMON DIP & SPREAD

16 oz. cream cheese, softened
1 lb. fresh salmon fillet
1 T. fresh parsley, chopped
2 T. finely chopped sweet onion
1 T. capers
1/4 c. mayonnaise

1/4 tsp. liquid smoke
2 tsp. Tabasco sauce
1 tsp. Worcestershire sauce
1 T. Paul Prudhomme's Seafood Magic

Put capers, onion, parsley, liquid smoke, Tabasco sauce, Worcestershire sauce and Seafood Magic in a food processor and process until almost liquid. Set mixture aside. Steam salmon fillet for about 15 minutes. (Your fish market can do this for you.) Remove skin and throw away. Blot fillet dry with paper towels and process in food processor for 10 seconds. Combine mayonnaise, cream cheese, processed sauce mixture and salmon in a mixing bowl and mix on high speed until all ingredients are well blended. Makes about 3 pounds and can be stored in refrigerator up to 7 days. Spread on your toasted bagel and you won't go back to lox.

23179-98

SMOKED SHRIMP DIP

16 oz. cream cheese, softened	¼ c. mayonnaise
½ lb. steamed, peeled & deveined shrimp	½ tsp. liquid smoke
	2 T. Texas Pete's hot sauce
1 T. fresh chopped parsley	1 tsp. Worcestershire sauce
2 T. finely chopped sweet onion	1 T. Paul Prudhomme's Seafood
1 T. capers	Magic

Put capers, onion, parsley, liquid smoke, Texas Pete sauce, Worcestershire sauce and Seafood Magic in a food processor and process until almost liquid. Set mixture aside. Combine shrimp, mayonnaise, cream cheese and processed sauce mixture in a mixing bowl and mix on high until all ingredients are well blended. Makes about 2 pounds and can be stored in refrigerator up to 7 days. This is the Queen of all my dips.

CAJUN TUNA DIP

16 oz. cream cheese, softened	½ tsp. liquid smoke
½ lb. fresh tuna	2 T. Texas Pete's hot sauce
1 T. fresh chopped parsley	1 tsp. Worcestershire sauce
2 T. finely chopped sweet onion	1 T. Paul Prudhomme's Seafood
1 T. capers	Magic
¼ c. mayonnaise	

Put capers, onion, parsley, liquid smoke, Texas Pete's sauce, Worcestershire sauce and Seafood Magic in a food processor and process until almost liquid. Set mixture aside. Steam tuna until well done. [Your seafood market can probably do this for you.) Place tuna in food processor and process very fine. Combine mayonnaise, cream cheese, processed sauce mixture and tuna in a mixing bowl and mix on high speed until all ingredients are well blended. Makes about 3 pounds and can be stored in refrigerator up to 7 days. This is a party hit.

SALMON LOG

1 lb. fresh salmon fillet	1 tsp. prepared horseradish
8 oz. cream cheese, softened	½ c. chopped pecans
1 T. lemon juice	3 T. finely chopped fresh parsley
1 tsp. grated Vidalia onion or Bermuda onion	1 T. capers, chopped

(continued)

23179-98

Steam salmon fillet for 15 minutes. Allow to cool. Remove skin. Blot with paper towel and flake. Add cream cheese, lemon juice, onion, capers, horseradish, and liquid smoke; mix well. Chill in refrigerator for 8 hours (overnight is ideal). Shape salmon mixture into a log. Combine pecans and parsley and mix well. Roll Salmon Log in pecan and parsley mixture. Chill for 4 to 6 hours. Serve log with crackers.

TUNA BITES

2 lbs. fresh tuna loin
2 c. seafood breader (I use House of Autry; mildly hot)

½ c. ginger teriyaki sauce
2 c. milk
1 c. corn oil

Cut tuna into bite-sized chunks and marinate in milk for 30 minutes. Heat oil to 375°. Put seafood breader in plastic bag. Remove tuna from milk. Shake off excess milk and drop about ½ pound at a time into plastic bag. Shake bag to coat tuna with breader. Drop coated fish into oil about ¼ pound at a time and cook until golden brown. Drain on paper towel. Serve with ginger teriyaki sauce for dipping. Serves 4 as a main course.

SHRIMPY DEVILED EGGS

12 hard-boiled eggs
½ lb. steamed shrimp
¼ c. sweet relish
½ tsp. dry mustard

¼ tsp. white pepper
½ tsp. salt
2 T. mayonnaise
1 T. chopped fresh parsley

Cut eggs in half and remove the yolks. Put shrimp in food processor and process for 10 seconds. Put egg yolks in processor and run processor for another 5 seconds. Combine yolk, and shrimp mixture in a bowl with relish, mustard, pepper, salt, mayonnaise and parsley. Fill egg whites with mixture. Makes 24 appetizers.

COCONUT SHRIMP

30 lg. shrimp
¾ c. self-rising flour
1 T. sugar
¾ c. beer

¾ c. all-purpose flour
2½ c. sweetened flaked coconut (I use Peter Paul brand)

(continued)

3

Peel shrimp leaving tail section of shell on. Mix sugar, beer and self-rising flour and set aside. Coat shrimp with all-purpose flour, dip into mixture and roll in flaked coconut. Pour 3 to 4 inches canola oil or peanut oil into a 2-quart saucepan and heat to 375°. Cook 4 to 6 shrimp at a time for 1 to 2 minutes. Drain on paper towels.

OYSTER FRITTERS

1 c. bacon fat & 1 c. corn oil or 2
  c. corn oil
1 c. self-rising flour
¼ c. self-rising cornmeal
½ tsp. salt

1 egg, slightly beaten
Kernels from 1 ear fresh corn
1 green onion, minced
½ pt. oysters, drained

Heat fat and oil in a 2-quart saucepan to 375°. Chop drained oysters and combine with flour, cornmeal, salt, egg, corn and green onion. Stir until just mixed. You should be able to form a a moist, sticky ball using 2 spoons; if too thin add more flour, it too thick add water. Drop by rounded tablespoonfuls into hot oil and cook until golden brown. Drain on paper towels. Makes 20 to 24 fritters.

STUFFED JALAPEÑO PEPPERS

14 lg. jalapeño peppers
½ crab dressing recipe
2 c. corn oil

½ c. all-purpose flour
¾ c. beer

Cut peppers in half starting just below the stem. Leave the stem on the pepper and both sides joined together at the top. Very carefully remove the seed pods. Place the pepper in a medium saucepan and cover with cold water. Bring to a simmer and drain. Repeat this process 1 more time. Dry the peppers with paper towels, being careful not to tear the pepper halves apart. Fill the inside of the peppers with the crab dressing and press the halves together. Place in a dish, cover and chill for 1 hour. Place flour in a bowl and slowly whisk in beer. Let stand for 30 minutes. Heat oil in a 2-quart pot to 375°. Holding the peppers by the stems, 1 at a time, dip in batter to coat. Drop into hot oil a few at a time (do not crowd) and cook to a golden brown. Drain on paper towels and serve with hot mustard sauce for dipping.

23179-98

ICED TEA COCKTAIL

1 c. boiling water
2 tea bags
½ c. sugar
4 c. ice water

½ c. lime juice
2½ c. orange juice
8 sprigs of mint or lime slices

Pour boiling water over tea and let stand 3 minutes. Remove tea bags. Stir in sugar until dissolved. Add ice water and fruit juices. Pour into 8 ice filled ice tea glasses and garnish each with a sprig of mint or lime slice.

BUTTERED RUM WITH AN OUTER BANKS FLAIR

2 c. apple cider
1 T. fresh lemon juice
1 T. fresh lime juice
30 to 35 whole allspice berries
6 whole cloves

1 crushed cinnamon stick
1 tsp. honey
1½ T. unsalted butter
2 shots dark rum

Combine all ingredients except rum in a saucepan and boil for 5 minutes. Strain and pour into 2 warm mugs. Add 1 shot of rum to each mug and serve. Makes 2 servings. Add more rum if you like.

EGG NOG

2 eggs, beaten
4 T. sugar
¼ tsp. salt

4 c. cold milk
¼ tsp. vanilla
¼ tsp. fresh grated nutmeg

Combine egg, sugar, salt and nutmeg and beat until sugar dissolves. Add milk and vanilla and beat well. Refrigerate for 4 hours. Stir and serve. Makes 4 servings.

23179-98

Recipe Favorites

Soups,
Salads
&
Vegetables

Helpful Hints

- Fresh lemon juice will remove onion scent from hands.

- To save money, pour all leftover vegetables and water in which they are cooked into a freezer container. When full, add tomato juice and seasoning to create a "free" soup.

- Three large stalks of celery, chopped and added to about two cups of beans (navy, brown, pinto, etc.), will make them easier to digest.

- When cooking vegetables that grow above ground, the rule of thumb is to boil them without a cover.

- A lump of sugar added to water when cooking greens helps vegetables retain their fresh color.

- Never soak vegetables after slicing; they will lose much of their nutritional value.

- Fresh vegetables require little seasoning or cooking. If the vegetable is old, dress it up with sauces or seasoning.

- To quickly bake potatoes, place them in boiling water for 10 to 15 minutes. Pierce their skins with a fork and bake in a preheated oven.

- To cut down on odors when cooking cabbage, cauliflower, etc..., add a little vinegar to the cooking water.

- To avoid tears when cutting onions, try cutting them under cold running water or briefly placing them in the freezer before cutting.

- A little vinegar or lemon juice added to potatoes before draining will make them extra white when mashed.

- To avoid toughened beans or corn, add salt midway through cooking.

- For an easy no-mess side dish, try grilling your vegetables along with your meat.

- To dress up buttered, cooked vegetables, sprinkle them with toasted sesame seeds, toasted chopped nuts, canned french-fried onions or slightly crushed seasoned croutons.

Soups, Salads & Vegetables

DOWN HOME POTATO SALAD

5 c. potatoes, peeled & diced
1½ T. sugar
1½ tsp. salt
½ c. chopped bread & butter
   pickles
½ c. chopped celery

½ c. chopped onions
½ c. mayonnaise
½ c. Marzetti slaw dressing
1 hard-boiled egg, sliced
3 hard-boiled eggs, chopped
Pimentos

Cook potatoes in a large pot with 2 quarts of water, until tender. Drain and set aside to cool. Combine pickle, celery, onions, mayonnaise and slaw dressing; mix well. Combine with potatoes and chopped eggs. Transfer to serving dish; garnish with sliced egg and pimentos. Serves 8 to 10.

Virgie Cox
Mother

LIGHT KEEPERS STEW

(Beef Stew)

3 c. dry red wine
3 c. beef stock or canned beef
   broth
7 garlic cloves, chopped
4 onions, chopped
3 carrots, chopped
¾ c. olive oil
½ c. brandy
¼ c. red wine vinegar
4 lbs. boneless beef chuck, cut
   into 1-inch pieces

½ c. peeled whole garlic cloves
8 anchovy fillets, chopped
3 T. drained capers
3 T. chopped cornichons (or
   capers)
Cooked rice
Bouquet garni (6 parsley stems, 6
   thyme sprigs, 6 bay leaves;
   wrapped & tied in cheese cloth)

Combine wine, stock, 3 chopped garlic cloves, 3 chopped onions, carrots, ½ cup oil, brandy and bouquet Garni in bowl; add beef, cover and chill in refrigerator for 12 hours. Heat remaining ¼ cup of oil in a large pot over medium heat. Add remaining chopped onions and chopped garlic and sauté until onions are tender and golden. Add beef, marinade and whole garlic cloves. Cover and simmer 2 hours until beef is tender. Drain cooking liquid from beef into heavy large saucepan. Discard bouquet garni. Skim grease from top of liquid. Boil until reduced to about 2 cups. Pour sauce over meat. Heat stew over medium heat. Stir

(continued)

7

in anchovies, capers and cornichons. Simmer for 10 minutes. Season to taste with salt and pepper. Serve over rice. Makes 4 to 5 servings.

GARLIC & POTATO SOUP

3 c. chicken or shrimp stock	1¼ c. milk
2½ c. peeled & diced potatoes	½ stick butter, softened
2 whole garlic bulbs, separated & peeled	1½ tsp. finely chopped fresh rosemary

Combine garlic, chicken stock and potatoes in a large saucepan and bring to a boil. Reduce to medium heat and cook until potatoes are tender, stirring occasionally. Takes about 15 minutes. Purée in blender or food processor. Return to saucepan and stir in milk. Season with salt and pepper. Mix butter and rosemary until well blended. Ladle soup into 4 bowls and top with a small dollop of rosemary butter.

BOUILLABAISE

2 lbs. red snapper, haddock, tile fish or grouper	1 lg. Vidalia or Bermuda onion, finely chopped
¾ lb. shrimp, lobster, scallops, crabmeat or combination of all to make ¾ lb. (I recommend a combination of all)	2 shallots, minced
	4 cloves garlic, minced
	1 (13-oz.) can tomatoes with liquid
	2 tsp. salt
8 sm. clams, 10 sm. mussels, 16 blue crab (or 8 stone crab) claws & ½ pt. oysters	Dash cayenne (⅛ tsp.)
	½ tsp. each thyme, basil, saffron & chopped parsley
¼ c. olive oil	

Cut fish into bite-sized pieces. Scrub clams and mussels well. I recommend purging the clams as follows: Place scrubbed clams in enough water to cover them and add 1 tablespoon cornmeal to water. Let stand for 1 hour, then drain. They are ready for use. Heat oil, sauté onions, shallots and garlic about 10 minutes or until onions become translucent. Add liquid, tomatoes and seasoning, except parsley. Lower heat and simmer 15 minutes. Add all seafood. Cover and cook 10 minutes. Serve in large bowl; sprinkle a lot of fresh parsley over the top. Serve with crusty bread. Makes 6 servings.

23179-98

PAELLA
(Piɛ-ʌlʌ)

1 tsp. saffron (this is very
expensive spice; you may omit
it, but if you do the dish will not
be as good or authentic)
¾ tsp. oregano
1 tsp. salt
1 coarse chopped green pepper
1 chopped sm. chili pepper
2 celery stalks, chopped
4 garlic cloves, minced fine
4 med. green onions with tops,
chopped
2 c. rice
½ lb. chorizo sausage

2 whole chicken breasts, split,
halved & quartered
¼ c. olive oil
10 chicken thighs
1 can artichoke hearts, cut in half
30 med. to lg. (raw) shelled &
deveined shrimp
4 c. chicken broth
15 to 18 fresh clams, cleaned &
purged
20 mussels, washed & beards
removed
1 sm. monk fillet, cubed

Heat olive oil in large frying pan over medium heat. Brown chicken pieces on all sides and drain on paper towels. Brown chorizo sausage and drain on paper towels. Drain the frying pan leaving about ¼ cup oil. Add onions, celery, garlic and rice. Sauté on medium heat until rice is golden brown. Add salt, saffron, oregano, chicken stock and artichoke hearts; simmer for 5 minutes. Pour mixture into a large shallow oven-proof dish. Caution; this mixture should not be closer than 1 inch from top of dish, if it is use 2 dishes. Place chicken pieces and fish pieces on top of rice. Press fish pieces into mixture. Cover with aluminum foil and bake at 350° for 20 minutes. Remove from oven, arrange shrimp, clams and mussels on top of rice mixture. Cover and return to oven to bake an additional 10 minutes. Serve with Cuban bread. Makes 10 servings.

SHRIMP BISQUE

½ lb. shelled, deveined raw
shrimp
1 c. unseasoned mashed potatoes
1 sm. chile pepper, chopped fine
1 qt. whole milk
2 c. shrimp stock (may substitute
for chicken stock)

½ tsp. salt
¼ tsp. black pepper
1 green onion, chopped fine
2 T. butter
1 bay leaf
Grated cheddar cheese

Melt butter in a 3-quart saucepan over medium heat, add onion and sauté until tender. Add stock, salt and bay leaf. Reduce heat and add

(continued)

9

mashed potatoes. Stir until hot and well blended. Add chopped chile. Coarsely chopped shrimp and add to pot. Simmer for 3 minutes. Add milk and bring back to a simmer. Remove from heat and serve in bowls. Garnish with grated cheese. Serves 6.

CHEF DIRT'S SMOKED SALMON BISQUE

2 T. butter	1½ c. chicken broth
1 lb. smoked salmon, skin	2 c. heavy cream
removed and broken up	¼ c. dry sherry
4 slices bacon	¼ tsp. salt
1 T. minced onion	¼ tsp. thyme
1 garlic clove, pressed	Pinch fresh ground nutmeg
2 T. all-purpose flour	

Chop bacon and cook in a skillet until crisp. Remove bacon from skillet and set aside. Drain excess grease from skillet. Sauté onion and garlic, in skillet used to cook bacon, over medium heat until tender, about 4 minutes. Sprinkle evenly with flour and cook stirring constantly, one minute. Gradually add chicken broth; cook over medium heat, stirring constantly, 4 to 5 minutes. Stir in salmon, bacon, cream, salt, butter, thyme and sherry. Cook 8 to 10 minutes or just until thoroughly heated (DO NOT BOIL). Sprinkle fresh ground nutmeg over the top and serve. Makes about 6½ cups.

COLD DAY SEAFOOD CHOWDER

2 T. tomato paste	1 c. shrimp or chicken stock
1 (6½-oz.) can chopped clams	½ tsp. Italian seasoning
1 (8-oz.) bottle clam juice	¼ tsp. cayenne pepper
1 lb. red snapper fillets, cut into	2 T. olive oil
1-inch pieces	1 med. onion, sliced
½ lb. raw med. shrimp, peeled &	2 garlic cloves, chopped
deveined	1 stalk celery, chopped
¼ lb. bay scallops	1 med. potato, cubed (sm.)
1 (10¾-oz.) can tomato soup	1 bay leaf
2 T. minced fresh parsley	

Heat oil in heavy large saucepan over medium high heat. Add onion, celery and garlic and sauté until onion is tender (about 10 minutes). Drain clams, reserving liquid. Add liquid and shrimp stock to saucepan. Stir in tomato soup, clam juice and tomato paste and bring to a boil. Add

(continued)

fish, shrimp, scallops, parsley, bay leaf, Italian seasoning and cayenne. Simmer 3 to 4 minutes. Stir in clams; simmer 1 more minute. Salt and pepper to taste. Makes 4 to 6 servings.

CLAM CHOWDER

Not to be confused with Manhattan or New England Chowder; this is a southeast version.

2 c. dice potatoes
1 (32-oz.) can or 30 to 40 cherry stone clams
½ lb. salt pork, cubed ½ inch
½ c. chopped celery

½ c. chopped onions
¼ tsp. black pepper
½ tsp. salt
¼ tsp. fresh thyme
1 bay leaf

Drain clams, reserving liquid. Combine clam liquid, celery, potatoes, onions, pepper, thyme, bay leaf, salt pork, potatoes in large stockpot. Make sure ingredients are covered about 3 inches with liquid (if not add water); cover pot and simmer until potatoes are done. Remove salt pork and bay leaf and discard. Chop clams and add to stockpot. Heat until just hot and serve. **Caution:** Over cooking will toughen clams. Makes 6 servings.

CHICKEN AND CORN CHOWDER

3 ears fresh corn or 1 (10-oz.) pkg. frozen whole kernel corn, thawed
2 T. butter
1 sm. onion, minced
6 c. water
1 tsp. sugar

1½ tsp. salt
2 c. heavy cream
1 sm. chicken (about 2 pounds), cut up
¼ tsp. fresh grated nutmeg
1 T. fresh grated parsley

Place chicken in a large pot with water. Cook until tender. Remove chicken pieces from pot and allow to cool. Skim fat from cooking liquid and reserve 3 cups of liquid. Remove chicken from bone and dice. Combine chicken and reserved liquid back into pot. Sauté onion in butter in a small sauté pan or skillet. Add to chicken pot mixture. Add corn, sugar, salt, parsley and nutmeg. Bring to a boil, reduce heat to a simmer and cook for 5 minutes. Stir in heavy cream. Heat until hot but do not allow to boil. Serve. Serves 4 to 6.

23179-98

TOMATO DUMPLINGS

¼ c. butter
½ c. diced onion
¼ c. diced green bell pepper
¼ c. diced celery
1 bay leaf
1 (28-oz.) can whole tomatoes
½ tsp. salt
¼ tsp. black pepper
1 c. all-purpose flour (I use
    Southern Biscuit)

2 tsp. baking powder
1 T. butter
1 egg, lightly beaten
⅓ c. milk
1 T. minced fresh parsley
Grated fresh nutmeg
½ tsp. salt

In a saucepan, melt ¼ cup butter. Add the onion, bell pepper, celery and bay leaf. Cook over medium high heat for 3 minutes (do not burn the butter). Stir in the tomatoes, salt and pepper. Bring to a boil, reduce heat and simmer for 4 minutes. In a large bowl, combine flour, baking powder and ½ teaspoon salt. Cut 1 tablespoon butter into this mixture until mixture is like cornmeal. Add egg, milk and parsley. Stir until dry ingredients are just moistened. (Do not knead as you would biscuits.) Drop dough mixture into simmering tomato mixture by the spoonfuls (using two tablespoons form into balls). Cover and cook over medium low heat for 20 minutes. (Allow to cook tightly covered, no peeking!) Sprinkle fresh ground nutmeg over dish before serving (about ⅛ teaspoon). Makes 5 servings. **Note:** Do not try to keep this dish hot for a prolonged period of time. Dumplings will overcook and fall apart.

SLICED TOMATO PESTO

5 lg. tomatoes, cut into ½-inch
    thick slices
1 T. lemon zest
1 c. chopped parsley
½ c. chopped green onions with
    tops

2 garlic cloves, crushed
½ c. olive oil
1 c. fresh basil leaves

Combine onions, parsley, garlic and basil in food processor. With processor running gradually add olive oil and blend until smooth. Add salt and pepper to taste. Refrigerate for at least 8 hours (overnight is better). Arrange tomato slices on serving plate and spoon pesto mixture over tomatoes. Let set at room temperature for 30 minutes and serve.

23179-98

CAESAR SALAD

1 head romaine lettuce, torn into
   pieces
16 to 20 sm. spinach leaves
Juice from 1 fresh lemon
1 tsp. Dijon mustard
2 cloves garlic, crushed

3 drops Worcestershire sauce
4 anchovy fillets, chopped
3 T. olive oil
Salt & pepper to taste
1 egg
1 c. garlic flavored croutons

Combine lettuce and spinach leaves in large bowl and set aside. Combine mustard, garlic, Worcestershire sauce, anchovy, olive oil, mustard and lemon juice in a medium-size mixing bowl. Plunge egg into boiling water for only 45 seconds. Crack egg and allow only the runny part to drop into salad dressing bowl. Beat well with other salad dressing ingredients. Combine croutons and lettuce and toss; pour over salad dressing and toss again. Serve on chilled plates. Serves 4 to 6.

WALDORF SALAD

Fresh parsley (opt.)
2 Golden Delicious apples
2 Jonathan or Red Delicious
   apples
½ c. diced celery
6 oz. red grapes (seedless),
   halved
½ c. walnuts, coarsely chopped

¼ c. pecans, coarsely chopped
¼ c. almonds, sliced
1 c. mayonnaise (I use Dukes)
1 T. fresh lemon juice
3 T. + 1 tsp. heavy cream

Core and dice apples; combine with celery, nuts, grapes and lemon juice and toss. Combine mayonnaise and cream in a bowl and whip. Pour dressing over salad and fold. Garnish with fresh parsley if desired. Makes 6 servings.

WATERCRESS & ORANGE SALAD

3 bunches washed & stripped
   watercress
Segments from 4 fresh oranges
Zest from 1 orange (about 1 T.)
6 T. peanut oil

¼ c. fresh squeezed orange juice
⅛ tsp. sugar
1 tsp. lemon juice
Pinch of salt & pepper

Tear watercress into salad pieces. Arrange a bed of watercress on 4 chilled plates with orange slices placed on top. Combine oil, orange

(continued)

juice, lemon juice, and sugar in a bowl and blend with a wire whip. Pour over salad plates or serve on the side. Provide salt and pepper for taste.

BIRD OF PARADISE SALAD

1 c. white seedless grapes	¼ c. finely chopped celery
4 chicken breast halves (skinless, boneless & cooked)	¼ c. finely chopped Vidalia onion
⅛ tsp. tarragon	⅛ tsp. cinnamon
¼ c. sliced almonds	6 peach halves
½ c. honey	Butter or Bibb lettuce
	½ c. grated mild cheddar cheese

Dice chicken and mix with tarragon, almonds, honey, celery, onion, cinnamon, honey and grapes. Arrange lettuce on 6 chilled plates to make a bed. Place a peach half into the center of each lettuce bed. Spoon chicken salad into peach half and top with grated cheese.

Chef Sonny Bear
Kill Devil Hills, NC

COLESLAW

1 c. shredded white cabbage	¼ c. shredded carrot
1 c. shredded red cabbage	½ c. Marzetti coleslaw dressing
½ tsp. celery seed	

Combine all ingredients; toss and refrigerate for 1 hour before serving. Makes 6 to 8 servings.

SWEET & SOUR COLESLAW
(Make The Day Before)

1 med. cabbage, shredded	1 tsp. celery seed
1 sm. onion, grated	⅓ tsp. caraway seed
¾ c. sugar	1 tsp. dry mustard
¾ c. vinegar	1 tsp. salt
¼ c. olive oil	⅛ tsp. white pepper

Mix together cabbage and onion in a large bowl and set aside. Combine sugar, vinegar, oil, celery seed, caraway seed, dry mustard, salt and pepper in a medium saucepan. Boil for 3 minutes; let cool to warm.

(continued)

23179-98

Pour over cabbage; toss well. Chill overnight in refrigerator. Makes 8 servings.

TUNA SALAD
(The Worlds Best)

2 lbs. fresh tuna, steamed well done	1 tsp. white pepper
16 oz. sweet salad cubes, drained	½ tsp. salt
½ c. finely chopped onions	1 T. capers
½ c. finely chopped celery	¾ c. mayonnaise (I use Dukes)
	4 oz. diced pimentos, drained

Flake tuna and mix well using your hands with all ingredients. Store in refrigerator up to 7 days. Makes 4 pounds and won't last long. Everyone's favorite.

SHRIMP SALAD

1 lb. fresh peeled, deveined cooked med. shrimp	⅔ c. finely chopped onion
2 T. finely chopped fresh parsley	1 T. diced pimentos
2 T. minced shallots	⅔ c. finely chopped celery
¼ c. fresh lemon juice	2 cloves garlic, minced
¼ c. Dijon mustard	⅛ tsp. cayenne pepper
2 T. prepared horseradish	¾ c. olive oil
2 tsp. paprika	Lettuce

Whisk lemon juice, mustard, horseradish, paprika, cloves and cayenne pepper in a bowl until well combined. Gradually add oil, whisking constantly until mixture thickens. Stir in celery, onion, shallot and parsley. Salt and pepper to taste. Place shrimp in a large bowl and pour on enough dressing to coat. Cover and refrigerate for 2 hours. Arrange a bed of lettuce on 4 chilled plates. Spoon shrimp salad over lettuce bed and serve with reserved dressing on the side.

23179-98

FRIED SUMMER SQUASH

2 T. oil
1 sliced sm. onion
8 sm. yellow squash, cut into
  1/4-inch thick slices

1/2 tsp. salt
1/4 tsp. black pepper
1 T. chopped fresh parsley

Heat oil in a large heavy skillet over medium heat. Add onion and sauté until just tender. Add squash and salt and pepper. Reduce heat, cover and simmer 10 minutes. Add parsley and continue to cook another 5 minutes. Serves 4.

OUTER BANKS CARROTS

4 c. sliced raw carrots
1 1/4 c. sliced onions, separated
  into rings
1/8 tsp. white pepper
2 T. chopped parsley
1/8 tsp. salt

1 T. brown sugar
1/2 tsp. ground nutmeg
1/8 tsp. ground cloves
1/2 c. unsweetened pineapple juice
2 T. margarine

Melt margarine in a 2-quart or larger saucepan. Add all ingredients except parsley; cover and simmer 15 minutes. Top with parsley and serve. Makes about 8 servings.

CREAMED PEAS

2 c. fresh or frozen peas
1 T. all-purpose flour
1 T. minced onion
1/2 tsp. salt

1/2 stick, butter
2 c. water
1 1/2 c. milk

Combine peas, salt and water in a 2-quart saucepan and cook over medium high heat until peas are tender. Drain and set aside. Combine butter, milk, onion and flour and simmer over medium heat, whisking continuously until slightly thickened. Add peas and continue to simmer for 3 to 5 minutes. Remove from heat and serve. Makes 4 to 6 servings.

23179-98

CORN IN BUTTER SAUCE

4 c. frozen shoe peg corn   ½ tsp. salt
1 stick butter   2 T. all-purpose flour

Heat corn over medium low heat in a medium saucepan until hot. Melt butter, remove from heat, add flour and salt and mix well. Add butter mixture to hot corn and mix well. Serve warm. Serves 6 to 8.

EASY CORN ON THE COB

Shuck ear of corn and remove silks; wet. Wrap ear in 3 paper towels. Wet paper towels. Place in microwave oven, cook for 90 seconds. Turn 180° and cook for another 60 seconds. Corn will retain more flavor and vitamins and minerals will not be cooked away in as in a pot of water. **Preparing Corn On The Cob For Grill:** Pull back shucks, remove silk. Break or cut off first inch of cob. Pull shucks back over ear of corn and tie ends with tie wraps. Place on medium hot part of grill. Turn often. Shucks will turn brown; corn will cook juicy and tender.

FRIED GREEN TOMATOES

3 lg. firm green tomatoes   1 c. milk
1 c. plain flour   1 tsp. salt
¼ c. cornmeal   ½ tsp. black pepper
1 egg, well beaten   ¼ c. bacon fat or lard

Slice green tomatoes into ⅜-inch thick slices. Combine egg and milk and mix well. Place tomatoes in a large bowl and pour egg wash over them. Heat fat in a large heavy skillet over medium heat. Combine flour, cornmeal, salt, and pepper and mix well. Remove tomatoes from egg wash 1 at a time allowing excess to drip back into bowl. Coat with flour/cornmeal mixture and fry until golden brown on each side. Drain on paper towels and keep hot. Makes servings 4 to 6.

23179-98

CARROTS & PINEAPPLE

About 1¼ lbs. carrots	1 T. brown sugar
¼ c. melted butter	1 tsp. salt
¼ c. pineapple juice	1 T. bourbon
1 c. pineapple chunks	¼ c. toasted sliced almonds

Cut carrots in half, then cut into ¼-inch thick strips. Place carrots in an ungreased 8 x 8 x 2-inch baking dish. Arrange pineapple chunks on top of carrots. Preheat oven to 375°°. Mix butter, pineapple juice, salt, sugar and bourbon. Pour mixture over carrots and pineapple. Place uncovered in oven for 40 minutes. Garnish with toasted almonds and serve. Serves 4.

CABBAGE & POTATOES

4 med. potatoes, peeled & cut into chunks (about 1-inch)	½ c. milk
	3 green onions, chopped
¾ lb. green cabbage, sliced thin	¾ stick unsalted butter, softened
½ + 4 T. water	

Cook potatoes in salted water; drain and mash and set aside. Combine cabbage and water in a large skillet. Cook about 15 minutes or until almost all of the liquid has evaporated. Combine potatoes and cabbage. Combine milk, onions, and ¾ of the softened butter in a medium saucepan and heat to a boil; stir and pour over cabbage and potato mixture. Stir to combine all ingredients. Place in a bowl. Make a well in the center of mixture; melt remaining butter and pour into well. Serve hot. Makes 2 servings. Great with corned beef.

BAKED VIDALIA ONIONS

6 lg. Vidalia onions	2 c. shredded sharp cheddar cheese
1 (6-oz.) pkg. cornbread stuffing mix	

Peel onions and cut a small slice from top and bottom. Cut each onion into wedges, cutting to within ½ inch of bottom. Set aside. Prepare stuffing mix according to package directions. Cool and stir in cheese. Fill onions with stuffing mixture and wrap each onion in aluminum foil. Place onions in a baking pan large enough to give at least 1 inch

(continued)

23179-98

clearance around each onion. Bake at 350° for 45 minutes. Makes 6 servings and is great for backyard cookouts.

MACARONI & TOMATOES

1 c. uncooked elbow macaroni	2 T. bacon fat
3 (10-oz.) cans diced tomatoes	1 tsp. salt
with green chiles	½ tsp. black pepper

Cook macaroni according to package directions. Drain and add all other ingredients. Heat until just hot and serve.

RICE PILAF

¼ c. chopped fresh parsley	1⅓ c. chicken broth
¼ c. green onions, sliced	1 T. vegetable oil
¼ c. mushrooms, sliced thin	½ c. uncooked long grain rice

Bring chicken broth to a boil in a 2-quart saucepan. Stir in rice; cover, reduce heat and simmer 20 to 25 minutes. Remove from heat. Heat oil in a small skillet. Sauté green onions and mushrooms until tender but still slightly crisp. Combine onions, mushrooms, and parsley with rice. Serve immediately. Makes 2 to 3 servings.

COUSCOUS
(Small Grain Shaped Pasta)

2 T. butter	2¼ c. chicken or shrimp broth
2 T. olive oil	2 c. couscous
3 green onions, minced	2 tsp. fresh parsley

Melt butter with oil in 2-quart saucepan over medium heat. Add onions and sauté 1 minute. Add broth and bring to a boil. Mix in couscous. Remove from heat. Cover and let stand 10 minutes. Fluff with fork. Season with salt and move to serving dish. Top with parsley. Serve hot. Makes about 6 servings.

23179-98

COUNTRY-STYLE GREEN BEANS

2 qt. canned or fresh green beans
(if canned drain liquid off, if
fresh add ¾ c. water)

¼ lb. country ham pieces

Combine beans and ham in a large saucepan. Cook over medium heat until all water has almost evaporated, about 30 minutes, stirring often; be very careful not to burn. (If using fresh green beans, simmer about 1½ hours.) Serves 6 to 8.

Virgie Cox
Mother

RECIPE FAVORITES

23179-98

*M*ain
Dishes
&
*C*asseroles

Helpful Hints

- When preparing a casserole, make an additional batch to freeze. It makes a great emergency meal when unexpected guests arrive. Just take the casserole from the freezer and bake it in the oven.

- To keep hot oil from splattering, sprinkle a little salt or flour in the pan before frying.

- Never overcook foods that are to be frozen. Foods will finish cooking when reheated. Don't refreeze cooked thawed foods.

- A few drops of lemon juice added to simmering rice will keep the grains separated.

- Green pepper may change the flavor of frozen casseroles. Clove, garlic and pepper flavors get stronger when they are frozen, while sage, onion and salt get milder.

- Don't freeze cooked egg whites; they become tough.

- Spray your grill with vegetable oil to prevent sticking.

- Instant potatoes are a good stew thickener.

- When freezing foods, label each container with its contents and the date it was put into the freezer. Store at 0°. Always use frozen cooked foods within one to two months.

- Store dried pasta, rice (except brown rice) and whole grains in tightly covered containers in a cool, dry place. Always refrigerate brown rice, and refrigerate or freeze grains if they will not be used within five months.

- Glazed pottery, earthenware, glass, metal - all can be used for casseroles. Many of these casserole containers come in bright colors and pleasing designs to complement your tableware. The type of container you use makes very little difference, as long as it is heatproof.

- Soufflé dishes are designed with straight sides to help your soufflé climb to magnificent heights. Ramekins are good for serving individual casseroles.

- To keep boiled lasagna noodles from sticking together as they cool, keep the noodles separate by draping them over the rim of a pot.

Main Dishes & Casseroles

STUFFED PEPPERS

¾ c. grated Swiss cheese
½ tsp. salt
3 lg. green bell peppers
1 can whole kernel corn, drained

½ c. diced onion
⅓ c. diced celery
1/ ¾ c. canned spaghetti sauce
1 lb. ground beef

Cut peppers in half lengthwise. Place in a 2-inch deep baking dish; set aside. Brown beef in a large skillet; drain off excess liquid. Combine onion, beef, corn, salt, meat sauce, and celery in a large bowl and mix. Spoon mixture into each pepper half. Bake in preheated 400° oven for 35 minutes. Garnish with grated cheese and bake another 3 minutes. Serves 6.

Virgie Cox
Mother

PRISSY JANE'S MACARONI & CHEESE

1¼ c. cooked shells macaroni
1 stick butter (¼ lb.)
1 T. finely chopped Vidalia or
  Bermuda onion
½ tsp. salt

¼ tsp. white pepper
¼ c. all-purpose flour
1¾ c. whole milk
8 oz. Velveeta or American
  cheese, cut into ½-inch cubes

Combine butter, onion, salt and pepper in a 2-quart saucepan. Heat over medium heat, stirring constantly, until onions are tender. Reduce heat to medium. Stir in flour. Stirring constantly, cook until smooth and bubbly. Pour in milk, stirring to boiling over medium heat. Remove from heat as soon as mixture reaches a slow boil. Stir in cheese until melted. Place macaroni in ungreased 1½-quart baking dish and stir in cheese mixture. Cook uncovered in a 375° oven for 30 minutes. Makes 4 generous servings. One little guy proved me wrong, he didn't get but 2 servings.

Sharon Swarmer
Daughter

23179-98

PEDRO'S PIZZA

6 oz. ground beef (lean)
1 c. grated cheddar cheese
¼ c. grated mozzarella cheese
1 c. grated Monterey Jack cheese
½-1.25-oz. pkg. taco seasoning mix
2 (10-inch) flour tortillas

1 c. seeded, chopped fresh tomatoes
2 sm. green onions, chopped
¼ c. sliced green olives
¼ c. sliced black olives
¾ c. sliced (thin) jalapeño peppers

Combine beef and taco seasoning mix in a large skillet and cook over medium heat until beef is brown and crumbled. Drain and set aside to cool. Heat a large iron skillet or griddle over high heat. Add 1 tortilla and cook for 30 seconds on each side. Cook second tortilla the same way. Reduce heat to medium, add cheddar cheese on top of tortilla in skillet. Top with other tortilla. As soon as cheese starts to melt, press down with spatula and cook for another 2 minutes. Preheat broiler. Remove to pizza pan. Top with beef mixture and then the Monterey Jack and mozzarella cheese. Place under broiler and cook until cheese melts (do not brown). Top with olives, onions, tomatoes and jalapeños. Cut into wedges and serve.

SHRIMP PIZZA

1 lb. med. shrimp, peeled and deveined
½ c. chopped green bell pepper
½ c. chopped onion
½ c. chopped celery
2 tsp. Creole seasoning
1 T. olive oil
⅔ c. roasted garlic sauce

1 (12-inch) refrigerated pizza crust (or your favorite one from a mix or homemade)
4 oz. shredded mozzarella cheese
¼ c. fresh grated Parmesan cheese

Combine oil, shrimp, bell pepper, onion, celery and Creole seasoning in a large skillet over medium heat, stirring constantly for 4 to 5 minutes or just until shrimp turns pink. Spread roasted garlic sauce over pizza crust. Top with shrimp mixture and cover with mozzarella and Parmesan cheese. Bake at 425° for 10 minutes.

23179-98

GROUND ROUND ON A BUN
(Sloppy Joes)

1 lb. lean ground round	1 (4-oz.) can tomato sauce
2 T. minced yellow onion	1 (5 to 6-oz.) can brown gravy
½ c. chopped fresh mushrooms	1 T. chili powder
1 tsp. Worcestershire sauce	½ tsp. salt
½ tsp. Tabasco sauce	6 hamburger buns or soft rolls

Cook ground beef and onion until browned. Crumble beef. Stir in mushrooms, Worcestershire sauce, Tabasco sauce, tomato sauce, brown gravy, chili powder and salt; simmer 10 minutes and spoon ground beef mixture on to rolls or buns, toast, or warm bread.

CREPE ROLL-UPS

1 c. self-rising flour (I use Southern Biscuit)	1 egg, well beaten
⅛ c. vegetable oil (about 2 T.)	¼ lb. pork sausage, cooked & crumbled
¼ tsp. vanilla extract	4 eggs, well beaten
1 T. sugar	4 to 6 slices American cheese, cut
½ to ¾ c. milk	into ¾-inch strips
Dash salt (about ⅛ tsp.)	Powdered sugar

Using a hot griddle prepare crepes as follows: Combine first 6 ingredients and mix just until batter has no lumps. Batter should be thick (or thin) as log cabin syrup (in my opinion as thin, runny). Add additional milk to achieve this texture. **Note:** Batter will thicken as it sets in bowl so you must continually thin it. Pour batter onto hot oiled griddle and tilt griddle back and forth and side to side to heat an 8-inch diameter crepe. Crepes will immediately start to form little bubbles all over the top; after about 30 seconds flip over and cook the other side. Crepes should be almost paper thin. Place each crepe on a paper towel and cover with another, stacking until all are cooked and set aside. In the center of each crepe make a ridge starting with cheese slices and building up to about 1 inch high by 1½ inches wide across the diameter of the crepe with scrambled egg and sausage. Fold 1 side of the crepe over the other. Starting from the fold, Roll the crepe up. Do this with all the crepes. Using melted butter, brush outside edges of rolled Crepe. Toast on all sides in a hot skillet. Garnish with powdered sugar and serve with dollops of butter and your favorite syrup.

23179-98

SURF, TURF & FEATHER

1 c. teriyaki sauce
4 cloves garlic minced
3 T. fresh lime juice
3 T. fresh minced ginger
2 T. dark brown sugar
1 lb. lg. shrimp (uncooked),
  peeled & deveined
1½ lbs. skinless chicken breasts,
  cut into ½-inch wide strips as
  long as you can make them

1¼ lb. beef skirt steak, cut into
  strips ¼-inch thick, ½-inch
  wide & about 3-inches long
Bamboo skewers (about 36,
  soaked in water for 1 hour)

Combine teriyaki, garlic, lime juice, ginger and sugar in a large bowl. Mix until sugar has dissolved. Place shrimp, chicken and beef in mixture and stir until well coated. Cover and marinate in refrigerator for 2 hours. Prepare grill to medium hot. Remove bowl from refrigerator and stir 1 last time. Thread each piece of chicken and beef on separate skewers (2 pieces to each skewer). Thread 3 shrimp to a skewer. Place skewers on grill and cook 3 minutes to each side. Serve with stir fry vegetables. Serves 6.

CHICKEN & DUMPLINGS A LA ANDREW

1 (2½ to 3-lb.) chicken
1 bay leaf
2 qt. water
½ tsp. black pepper

1 c. all-purpose flour
2 (10-count) cans biscuits
½ c. canned milk

Place chicken in large covered stockpot, at least 4-quart size. Add water, salt and bay leaf. Bring to a boil; cover and reduce heat. Simmer for 1 hour. Remove chicken and bay leaf from broth (discard bay leaf) and cool. Remove meat from bones and set aside. Do not chop or cut meat, but do cut breast into quarters. Cut each biscuit into quarters. Do not shake off excess flour, this will thicken the broth and make the gravy. Add canned milk to the broth and bring to a boil. Drop biscuit pieces into boiling broth a few at a time. Reduce heat to medium low and cook 8 to 10 minutes, stirring occasionally. Add chicken pieces and remove from heat. Cover and let stand 5 minutes before servings. Serves 4 to 6.

Andrew Milam
Grandson

23179-98

ONE POT

3 to 4 lb. chuck roast
2 med. onions, quartered
4 med. carrots, cut into 1-inch
  pieces
8 sm. potatoes, peeled
1 bay leaf

¼ tsp. black pepper
2 stalks celery, cut into 1-inch
  pieces
1 tsp. salt
2 T. oil
1 T. roux

Heat a large Dutch oven over low heat. Add oil. Place roast in Dutch oven and brown on both sides. Pour water into Dutch oven just to cover roast. Add salt, bay leaf, pepper and onions; cover and simmer for 1½ hours. Add potatoes and carrots; simmer until vegetables are tender. Remove roast, onion and carrots to serving platter and keep warm. Strain cooking liquid and return cooking liquid only to Dutch oven. Discard solids. Add roux to Dutch oven and heat until slightly thickened to make a sauce. Pour sauce over meat, potatoes, and carrots. Serve. Serves 4.

SAUSAGE GRAVY & BISCUITS

1 can biscuits (your favorite kind)
½ lb. fresh country sausage
2 c. skim milk

¼ tsp. black pepper
¼ tsp. salt
2 T. roux

Brown and crumble sausage in a medium skillet. Drain and set aside. Combine roux, milk, salt and pepper in a medium saucepan. Heat over medium heat, stirring continually as it thickens. Reduce heat, add sausage and simmer 5 minutes until hot. Bake biscuits according to directions. Place 2 biscuits in a plate and spoon hot gravy over them. Makes 4 to 5 servings.

23179-98

Recipe Favorites

Meat,
Poultry
&
Seafood

Helpful Hints

- Use little oil when preparing sauces and marinades for red meats. Fat from the meat will render out during cooking and will provide plenty of flavor. Certain meats, like ribs, pot roast, sausage and others, can be parboiled before grilling to reduce the fat content.

- When shopping for red meats, buy the leanest cuts you can find. Fat will show up as an opaque white coating, or can also run through the meat fibers, as marbling. Although most of the fat (the white coating) can be trimmed away, there isn't much that can be done about the marbling. Stay away from well marbled cuts of meat.

- Home from work late with no time for marinating meat? Pound meat lightly with a mallet or rolling pin, pierce with a fork, sprinkle lightly with meat tenderizer and add marinade. Refrigerate for about 20 minutes and you'll have succulent, tender meat.

- Marinating is a cinch if you use a plastic bag. The meat stays in the marinade and it's easy to turn and rearrange. Cleanup is easy; just toss the bag.

- It's easier to thinly slice meat if it's partially frozen.

- Tomatoes added to roasts will help to naturally tenderize them. Tomatoes contain an acid that works well to break down meats.

- Whenever possible, cut meats across the grain; they will be easier to eat and have a better appearance.

- When frying meat, sprinkle paprika over it to turn it golden brown.

- Thaw all meats in the refrigerator for maximum safety.

- Refrigerate poultry promptly after purchasing. Keep it in the coldest section of your refrigerator for up to two days. Freeze poultry for longer storage. Never leave poultry at room temperature for more than two hours.

- If you're microwaving skinned chicken, cover the baking dish with vented clear plastic wrap to keep the chicken moist.

- Lemon juice rubbed on fish before cooking will enhance the flavor and help maintain a good color.

- Scaling a fish is easier if vinegar is rubbed on the scales first.

Meat, Poultry & Seafood

RECOMMENDED MARINADES FOR BAKING, GRILLING OR BROILING FISH

Salmon - Lemon Butter Dill
Tuna - Ginger Teriyaki
Catfish - Cajun
Red Snapper - Lemon Butter Dill
Shark - Lemon Herb
Monk - Garlic Herb
Dolphin (Mahi-Mahi) - Lemon Herb

Tilapi - Lemon Butter Dill
Flounder - Mesquite
Swordfish - Lemon Butter Herb
Bluefish - Cajun
Tile Fish - Garlic Herb
Grouper - Lemon Herb

I use Golden Dip Brand but you will get much the same results by using your favorites.

Universal Marinades (use with any fish):

Italian Salad Dressing
Mayonnaise

Caper Sauce (recipe is in this book)

Marinades for grilled fish recipes in the book may be switched for any of the above.

DEEP FRIED FISH

2 lbs. fish fillets
Milk

Seafood breader (I use House of Autry)

Remove skin from fillets, using a very shape knife, by placing fillet skin side down on a flat surface and run the knife lengthwise between the skin and the meat or have the fish market do it for you. It is very important to remove the skin, or your fish won't taste as good. Pour about 2 cups milk into a deep bowl. Cut fish into chunks about 1½ to 2-inches square and drop into milk. Marinate fish in milk for 1 hour in the refrigerator. Put 2 cups seafood breader in a plastic bag. Drop a handful of fish chunks into plastic bag, first shake off excess milk. Shake plastic bag to coat fish, continue until all fish chunks have been coated. Heat 1 quart of corn oil in a 3-quart saucepan to 375°. Drop 6 to 7 fish chunks at a time into hot oil and cook until golden brown. Drain on paper towels. Serve with tartar sauce, cocktail sauce, cold slaw and hush puppies. Serves 4 to 6.

BAKED ROCK FISH

2 to 3 lbs. rock fish fillets
4 strips bacon
3 lg. washed potatoes, thinly
sliced

2 lg. onions, sliced ¼-inch thick
4 carrots, thinly sliced
Salt & pepper to taste

Place rock fish fillets in baking dish that has been lightly oiled. Salt and pepper fish. Put carrots and potatoes around and on top of fish and bake in preheated oven at 375° for 20 to 30 minutes. Serves 4 to 6.

BAKED PERCH

2 lbs. perch fillets
2 T. butter
2 limes, sliced very thin

1 tsp. paprika
1 T. chopped parsley

Place perch fillets, skin side down, in a 9 x 13-inch baking dish that has been lightly greased. Arrange lime slices over fillets and sprinkle with paprika. Bake in 350° preheated oven for 30 minutes. Garnish with parsley. Makes 4 servings.

CRAB CAKES

1 T. oil
1 lb. backfin crabmeat (remove shell)
1 T. Old Bay Seasoning
1 T. mayonnaise
1 T. chopped fresh parsley

¼ tsp. salt
½ tsp. Worcestershire sauce
¼ c. fresh bread crumbs
2 tsp. baking powder
1 egg, beaten
2 T. butter

Combine egg, baking powder, bread crumbs, Worcestershire sauce, salt, parsley, mayonnaise and Old Bay and mix well. Fold in crabmeat. Shape into 4 balls. Press gently to slightly flatten, about 1-inch thick. Melt butter in large frying pan and add oil. Heat over medium heat until hot. Very gently place crab cakes in frying pan and fry on each side 4 to 5 minutes or until golden brown. Do not push down with spatula while frying, **this is important!** Serves 2.

23179-98

DEVILED CRABS

1 lb. regular or back fin crabmeat, feel through crabmeat & remove shells
2 T. minced onions
2 T. minced celery
1 T. minced green pepper
3 T. chopped fresh parsley
1 T. Old Bay seasoning
3 eggs, beaten
4 c. fresh bread crumbs
1 tsp. Worcestershire Sauce
3 tsp. baking powder
½ tsp. Tabasco sauce
16 to 18 natural crab or aluminum shells

Combine and mix all ingredients well. Spoon into shells, heaping up in the center. Bake in a 400° preheated oven for 15 to 20 minutes until golden brown on top. **Note:** If you use natural shells, wash them in 1 part vinegar and 2 parts water.

CRAB STUFFED MUSHROOMS

24 lg. fresh mushrooms
1 lb. back fin crabmeat
½ tsp. Worcestershire sauce
2 tsp. Old Bay seasoning
1 T. mayonnaise
2 tsp. baking powder
1 egg, beaten
1 T. fresh chopped parsley
2 c. fresh bread crumbs
¼ lb. butter, melted
2½ T. grated Parmesan cheese

Clean mushrooms with a dry paper towel, do not wet mushrooms, and remove stems. Discard stems or save for another dish. Brush mushrooms with butter. Preheat oven to 375°. Combine ¼ cup of the bread crumbs, egg, parsley, baking powder, mayonnaise, Old Bay, and Worcestershire sauce in a medium-size bowl. Mix all ingredients until well blended, add crabmeat, toss to combine. Stuff each mushrooms with about 1 tablespoon of crabmeat mixture, add more as needed to use up all of mixture. Coat tops of stuffed mushrooms with bread crumbs. Drizzle a few drops of butter over each mushrooms and sprinkle with Parmesan cheese. Place in a shallow pan or cookie sheet. Mushrooms should not touch one another. Bake in preheated oven for 15 minutes. Serves 8 for a main course or 24 appetizers.

23179-98

TUNA SAUSAGE

2 lbs. fresh tuna	½ tsp. salt
½ lb. salt pork (rind removed)	½ tsp. oregano
½ tsp. nutmeg	½ tsp. caraway seed
½ tsp. black pepper	⅛ tsp. curry powder
1 tsp. crushed red pepper	2 T. fresh chopped parsley

Grind tuna and salt pork in meat grinder or food processor. Combine with nutmeg, black pepper, red pepper, salt, oregano, caraway seed, curry powder and parsley. Stuff into sausage casing for links (your butcher can furnish you with casings) or make into patties. Use and cook as you would any other sausage. Remember this is fish and it won't store anywhere near as long as regular sausage. Can be frozen up to 3 months.

POACHED SALMON

2 lbs. fresh salmon fillets	¼ c. chopped fresh parsley
2 tsp. cracked black pepper	1 T. salt
1 c. thinly sliced onions	2 qt. water
1 c. chopped celery tops	

Combine black pepper, onions, celery, parsley and salt in fish poacher or large roasting pan. Bring mixture in pan to a slow boil, reduce heat to medium. Place salmon in pan, cover and simmer for 10 minutes. Remove salmon from mixture to a warm serving platter. Cover with Hollandaise sauce and serve with steamed fresh asparagus. Serves 4.

TUNA REBECCA
(My Version Of Steak Diane Using Tuna Steaks)

½ tsp. salt	½ c. dry white wine
½ tsp. garlic powder	1 c. water
2 tsp. Worcestershire sauce	½ c. sliced fresh mushrooms
½ tsp. onion powder	2 (6 oz.) fresh yellow fin tuna
½ tsp. white pepper	steaks
1 T. butter	

Brush Worcestershire sauce over both sides of tuna steaks, sprinkle steaks with salt, garlic powder, onion powder and pepper. Refrigerate

(continued)

23179-98

for 1 hour. Melt butter in a large skillet. Add steaks. Cook over medium heat until browned, turning once. Pour wine over steaks. Cover. Reduce heat and simmer 15 minutes. Remove steaks to warm serving plate. Keep warm. Add 1 cup water and mushrooms to pan drippings. Boil uncovered, stirring frequently, about 10 minutes or until sauce is reduced to about ½ cup. Pour sauce over steaks and serve. Makes 2 servings.

MONK FISH KABOBS

1-1½ lbs. monk fish, cut into 16 pieces
8 strips bacon
8 very thin slices lemon, cut in half
1 green pepper, cut in 2-inch pieces

1 red pepper, cut in 2-inch pieces
8 bay leaves
12 mushroom caps
Peanut oil
Bearnaise sauce

Start kabobs by placing a piece of fish on each piece of bacon and top with a piece of lemon. Roll up and set aside. Place 1 piece of fish on a skewer; place 1 bay leaf next on skewer; next place 1 piece red pepper on skewer; next place a mushroom cap on a skewer; next place another piece of fish on skewer; next place 1 mushroom cap on skewer; next place 1 piece of fish on skewer; next place a bay leaf on skewer; next place 1 piece red pepper on skewer and finish with 1 piece fish. Repeat for 3 more skewers. Brush kabobs with peanut oil. Place on grill, cook 15 minutes, basting with oil and turning often. Salt and pepper to taste and serve with Bearnaise sauce. Makes 4 servings.

STEAMED MUSSELS

½ c. sliced carrots
½ c. sliced celery

2 c. white wine
4 lbs. mussels

Wash and debeard mussels. Combine all ingredients with mussels in a large covered pot. Bring pot to a boil. Remove from heat and let stand for 5 minutes. Serve mussels hot with warm butter for dipping.

23179-98

GRILLED GROUPER WITH MELON SALSA

¼ tsp. salt
½ c. fresh cantaloupe cubes (sm.)
½ c. honeydew melon cubes (sm.)
2 T. chopped fresh cilantro
2 T. fresh lime juice

½ tsp. lime zest
½ tsp. white pepper
2 (8-oz.) fillets grouper or red
   snapper
¼ c. Vidalia onion, chopped

Prepare grill for medium-high heat. Combine cantaloupe, melon cubes, onion, cilantro, lime juice, zest, salt and pepper. Toss. Cover and refrigerate for 1 hour. Brush fish fillet with oil. Place on grill for 3 minutes on each side. Place fillet on plates and spoon melon salsa over them. Makes 2 servings.

GRILLED SWORDFISH

2 (8-oz.) swordfish steaks
¼ c. olive oil
¼ c. melted butter
2 T. minced garlic

½ tsp. fresh dill
½ tsp. fresh ground black pepper
1 T. fresh parsley

Combine olive oil, garlic, dill, pepper, parsley, and salt in a large bowl and whip until well blended. Add swordfish steaks and marinate in refrigerator for 1 hour. Prepare grill for medium-high heat. Pour marinade in saucepan and heat with butter. Place fish on grill, cook 4 minutes on each side, basting frequently with marinade butter mixture. Serve hot. Makes 2 servings.

GRILLED RED SNAPPER

1 lb. red snapper fillets
2 tsp. chopped fresh mint
2 T. minced garlic
2 T. wine vinegar

¼ c. olive oil
1 tsp. salt
1 tsp. pepper
½ tsp. fresh dill

Combine olive oil, garlic, vinegar, mint, salt, pepper and dill in a bowl and mix well. Dredge fish in mixture, place on plate and set aside. Prepare grill for medium-high heat. Place fish on grill, skin side up. Cook 3 minutes. Turn and cook another 3 minutes. Brush remaining mixture on fish frequently while cooking. Makes 2 servings.

23179-98

GRILLED TUNA

2 (8 oz.) tuna steaks
1¼ c. mayonnaise
¼ c. teriyaki sauce

1 T. very finely minced fresh
ginger
1 garlic clove, minced fine

Combine mayonnaise, teriyaki, ginger and garlic in a large bowl and whip until well blended. Add tuna steaks and marinate in refrigerator for 1 hour. Prepare grill for medium-high heat. Drain marinade from bowl and reserve. Place tuna on grill, cook 4 minutes on each side, basting frequently with reserved marinade. Makes 2 servings.

GRILLED FLOUNDER

1 lb. flounder fillets
½ c. French dressing (bottled)
1 T. minced fresh parsley

2 tsp. minced fresh dill
2 tsp. minced fresh thyme
1 tsp. minced fresh basil

Combine French dressing, parsley, dill, thyme and basil in a large bowl. Whip until well blended. Add flounder fillets and marinate in refrigerator for 1 hour. Prepare grill for medium-high heat. Drain marinade from bowl and reserve. Place fillets skin side up on grill and cook for 3 minutes. Turn over and cook for an additional 3 minutes. Baste frequently while cooking with reserved marinade. Makes 2 servings.

GRILLED SHARK

2 (8 oz.) mako or black tip shark
steaks
¼ c. olive oil
2 T. fresh lemon juice
2 tsp. minced fresh basil

2 tsp. minced fresh oregano
2 cloves garlic, crushed & minced
2 tsp. fresh minced rosemary
1 T. fresh minced parsley
¼ tsp. each of salt & pepper

Combine olive oil, lemon juice, basil, oregano, garlic, rosemary parsley, salt and pepper in a large bowl. Whip until well blended. Add shark steaks and marinade in refrigerator for 1 hour. Prepare grill for medium-high heat. Drain marinade from bowl and reserve. Place shark steaks on grill. Cook 4 minutes on each side, basting frequently with reserved marinade. Makes 2 servings.

33

23179-98

GRILLED SALMON STEAKS

2 lg. salmon steaks (about ¾-inch thick)
1 stick butter
2 tsp. minced fresh dill
1 T. minced fresh parsley

1 tsp. fresh minced thyme
¼ tsp. black pepper
½ tsp. salt
½ fresh lemon

Prepare grill for medium-high heat. Melt butter and remove from heat. Combine with dill, parsley, thyme, salt and pepper. Baste both sides of steaks with mixture and place on grill. Cook 4 minutes on each side basting frequently. Move to hot serving plate and squeeze lemon on each steak. Makes 2 servings.

FRIED OYSTERS

1 pt. lg. select oysters
2 c. bread crumbs
½ tsp. salt
¼ tsp. black pepper

¼ c. flour
2 T. freshly chopped parsley
2 c. peanut oil

Combine bread crumbs, salt, pepper, flour, and parsley and mix well. Heat oil in a 2-quart saucepan to 375°. Coat each oyster in breading mix and drop a few at a time into the hot oil. Be very careful oil may pop out on you. Cook until golden brown; drain on paper towels and serve immediately. Serves 2.

FRIED SOFT SHELL CRABS

½ tsp. salt
6 soft shell crabs
1 egg
1 c. milk

2 c. fresh bread crumbs
¼ c. plain cornmeal
1 c. peanut oil
¼ tsp. black pepper

Combine egg and milk; beat well and set aside. Combine in plastic bag, salt, bread crumbs, cornmeal, and black pepper; shake bag well to mix all ingredients and set aside. Clean crabs or have the fish market do it for you. Marinate crabs in egg and milk wash for ½ hour in the refrigerator. Pour oil in a large frying pan and heat over medium heat. Remove crabs from wash and allow excess to drip back into bowl. Dredge crabs in the bread crumb mixture coating all surfaces, including legs and claws. Place crabs, 1 at a time and up to 3, in hot oil. Fry until

(continued)

34

23179-98

golden brown and crisp on each side, turning only once. Drain on paper towels and serve hot. Makes 3 servings.

ROCK ISLAND RED SNAPPER

2 lbs. red snapper fillets, skin
removed
½ tsp. white pepper
2 garlic cloves, crushed &
chopped very fine
1 T. fresh parsley, chopped very
fine

⅛ tsp. salt
1 T. fresh lemon juice
1 lb. unsalted melted butter
2 T. olive oil
2 T. melted butter

Combine pepper, garlic, parsley, salt, 2 tablespoons melted butter, lemon juice and oil and blend well. Preheat broiler. Cover a shallow pan with foil, baste fillets well with mixture and place in pan. Broil 3 inches from heat for 4 minutes, turn, baste again. Broil another 4 minutes. Heat 4 ramekins and pour ¼ cup warm butter in each; place 1 on each plate for dipping fork fulls of red snapper. Serves 4.

CRAWFISH & ANGEL HAIR PASTA

1 stick butter (¼ lb.)
3 cloves garlic, crushed &
chopped fine
1 lb. crawfish tails (can be bought
prepared & frozen)

12 oz. angel hair pasta
1 T. all-purpose flour
Grated Parmesan cheese

Cook pasta according to package directions. Melt butter over low heat. Add garlic, salt and flour. Heat, stirring constantly, until slightly thickened. If using frozen crawfish make sure they have been thawed and drained before starting. Add crawfish tails and heat until bubbly. Place pasta on warm serving platter; pour crawfish mixture over pasta and toss with Parmesan cheese. Serve with hot crust bread to sop up all the wonderful garlic butter sauce. Serves 4.

23179-98

WHITE CLAM SAUCE OVER PASTA

2 (4-oz. each) cans chopped
   clams
1 T. fresh chopped parsley
2 sticks butter (½ lb.)
½ c. olive oil

¼ tsp. salt
3 garlic cloves, minced very fine
8 oz. linguine or spaghetti
¼ c. Parmesan cheese, grated

Cook pasta according to package directions. Drain clams and reserve liquid. Combine olive oil, melted butter, garlic, salt and clam juice in food processor and mix for 15 seconds. Pour into a 1-quart saucepan. Add clams and simmer on medium heat for 5 minutes. Place warm pasta on a warm serving platter and pour clam sauce over pasta. Sprinkle Parmesan cheese and parsley over top and toss. Serve with crusty French bread. Serves 4 to 6.

CATFISH SUPREMA

1 pt. half & half
1 tsp. white pepper
¼ tsp. salt
2 tsp. all-purpose flour
⅛ tsp. garlic powder
2 T. butter
⅓ lb. peeled & deveined raw
   shrimp

1 lb. back fin crabmeat
6 to 8 sm. farm raised catfish
   fillets
Toothpicks
¼ c. Parmesan cheese
Sprigs of fresh parsley

Preheat oven to 400°. Combine half and half, pepper, salt, flour, garlic powder, butter and shrimp in a food processor and process for 10 seconds. Spread crabmeat over 1 side of fish. Roll each piece of fish with crabmeat jellyroll fashion and secure with toothpicks. Place in a 2-inch buttered baking dish and set aside. Add any remaining crab to the shrimp sauce. Spoon sauce over fish. Sprinkle Parmesan cheese over each piece of fish. Bake in preheated oven for 15 to 20 minutes. After baking remove from oven and transfer to warm serving dish. Whisk sauce from baking dish until well blended. Pour over fish. Garnish with fresh parsley and paprika. Serve hot. Serves 6.

23179-98

BUTTERFLY FRIED SHRIMP

¼ c. all-purpose flour
¼ c. cornstarch
⅛ tsp. salt
¼ c. beer
1 egg yolk

2 T. melted butter
1 lb. extra large shrimp (26-30 count)
Vegetable oil

Peel and devein shrimp **leaving last segment** and tail on. Cut shrimp down the back (vein side) to within ⅛ of an inch of the underside. Lay each shrimp, spread butterfly on a flat surface using the bottom of a large water glass; press down on shrimp until it lays flat. Shrimp is now completely butterflied. Combine flour, cornstarch, and salt in a small bowl. Add beer, egg yolk, and butter; beat until smooth. Dip shrimp into batter; deep fry in hot vegetable oil at 375° until golden brown. Makes 4 of the most delicious servings of fried shrimp you have ever had.

CRAWFISH OR SHRIMP CREOLE

2 T. oil
½ c. onions, chopped coarse
¾ c. celery, chopped coarse
¾ c. bell pepper, chopped coarse
2 c. chopped fresh tomatoes or 1 (16-oz.) can tomatoes
1 c. water (if using fresh tomatoes)
⅓ c. water (if using canned tomatoes)

½ tsp. crushed red pepper (1 tsp. if more heat is desired)
½ tsp. salt
¼ tsp. black pepper
2 T. roux
1 tsp. Tabasco sauce
1 lb. crawfish tails or raw peeled shrimp

In a large skillet or Dutch oven sauté onions, celery and bell pepper in oil until onions are tender. Add tomatoes, water, Tabasco, red pepper, salt and black pepper. Bring to a slow boil. Reduce heat and simmer for 10 minutes. Add roux, crawfish (or shrimp). Simmer for 5 more minutes, stirring continually until thickened. If too thick, add more water. Serve over cooked rice. Makes 4 to 6 servings.

23179-98

ISLAND GRILLED SHRIMP

1½ lb. extra large or jumbo
   shrimp
1 pinch (⅛ tsp.) powder ginger
1 pinch cinnamon
½ c. fresh orange juice
1 T. vinegar
1 T. fresh lime juice
1 fresh pineapple (cut into 1-inch
   chunks)

1 T. brown sugar
1 tsp. dry mustard
Flaked coconut
6 (10-inch) bamboo skewers
   (soaked in water for 15 minutes)

Alternately thread the pineapple and shrimp on to the skewers, 4 each to each skewer. Combine the remaining pineapple, ginger, cinnamon, orange juice, vinegar, lime juice, brown sugar and mustard in a food processor and process until liquid. Transfer mixture to saucepan, bring to a boil, reduce heat and simmer for 20 minutes. Allow mixture to cool. Baste shrimp and pineapple chunks with cool mixture. Let sit for 5 minutes, basting 2 more times while sitting. Prepare grill and adjust rack for medium high heat. Place skewers on rack and grill for 6 minutes, turning and basting often. Roll skewers in coconut to coat well. Heat remaining basting liquid and serve as a sauce.

SHRIMP AND SEASHELL PASTA WITH WINE AND CREAM SAUCE

1 lb. medium shrimp, peeled and
   deveined
1 garlic clove, pressed
¼ c. white wine (the kind you like
   to drink)
½ c. heavy cream
2 T. butter

¼ tsp. white pepper
½ tsp. salt
1 T. chopped fresh parsley
8 oz. seashell pasta
2 tsp. corn oil

Cook pasta according to package directions. Drain, rinse with cold water and set aside. Melt 1 tablespoon of butter with corn oil in a large heavy frying pan over medium high heat. Sauté shrimp just until they turn pink, about 2 minutes. Remove from skillet and set aside. Deglaze skillet with the wine; add the garlic, pepper and salt to the wine. Allow to cook for 30 seconds, reducing heat slightly and stirring constantly. Add the heavy cream and heat until mixture just starts to boil. Add the shrimp and pasta. Stir well and bring back to a simmer. Serve immediately. Serves 4.

23179-98

CRAWFISH ETUFEE

1 lb. cooked crawfish tail meat
2 tsp. Seafood Magic
1 T. flour
½ tsp. salt

2 T. oil
¼ c. diced onions
2 (10-oz.) cans diced tomatoes
with green chiles

Sauté onions in oil, add flour and blend with onions. Add Seafood Magic, salt, and tomatoes. Heat to simmer stirring constantly. Serve hot over cooked rice.

TUNA BURGERS

1 lb. fresh tuna
3 T. mayonnaise
1 T. butter
2 T. oil
3 American or cheddar cheese
slices

Salt & pepper
3 lg. soft rolls or hamburger buns,
toasted

Grind tuna in a food processor until it resembles ground beef. Remove tuna from processor and mix with mayonnaise. Shape into 3 (2½-inch) thick patties. Salt and pepper to taste. Heat oil and butter in large heavy skillet over medium heat. Cook for 4 minutes on each side. Place a slice of cheese on each pattie the last 2 minutes of cooking. Place on toasted bun and garnish with whatever makes you happy on hamburgers.

SEAFOOD LASAGNA

½ lb. crabmeat
½ lb. bay scallops
½ lb. raw med. shrimp, peeled &
deveined
1 (16-oz.) jar Alfredo sauce

1 c. broccoli florets
1 c. grated mozzarella cheese
1 c. ricotta cheese, drained
16 oz. cooked lasagna noodles

Coat the bottom of a 2 x 9 x 13-inch baking dish with ¼ cup alfredo sauce; layer lasagna noodles in bottom of dish; cover with scallops, ⅓ cup mozzarella, ⅓ cup broccoli, ⅓ cup Swiss and ⅓ cup ricotta cheese. Top this with ½ cup alfredo sauce. Start 2nd layer: Cover with layer of lasagna, cover with crab, cover with mozzarella, cover with ⅓ cup broccoli, cover with ⅓ cup Swiss and ⅓ cup ricotta cheese. Start 3rd

(continued)

23179-98

and final layer: Cover with layer of lasagna, cover with shrimp, cover with ⅓ cup broccoli, cover with ⅓ cup Swiss and ⅓ cup ricotta cheese. Top with 1 layer lasagna and remainder of alfredo sauce. Bake in 375° oven for 30 minutes. Remove from oven and let stand 10 minutes before cutting. Makes 6 generous servings.

SCALLOPS WITH SPARKLING WINE & SAFFRON

1 tsp. fresh lemon juice	⅛ tsp. saffron
¼ stick butter	1 c. whipping cream
20 to 25 sea scallops	⅛ tsp. white pepper
1½ c. dry sparking wine	¼ tsp. salt

Melt butter in large skillet over medium heat. Place scallops in pan and sauté 2 to 3 minutes. Transfer scallops to a plate and set aside. Add wine and saffron to skillet with scallop juices and boil until reduced to half of original. Add the cream and cook until slightly thickened, about 10 minutes. Add lemon juice, salt and pepper. Return scallops to skillet. Stir and heat 1 minute. Place in serving platter and garnish with fresh parsley. Makes 4 servings.

GARLIC SHRIMP WITH RED PEPPERS & MUSHROOMS

3 lg. red bell peppers	1½ lbs. med. raw shrimp,
6 garlic cloves, chopped	peeled & deveined
½ c. olive oil	2 T. fresh chopped parsley
12 oz. oyster mushrooms	
1 T. finely chopped red jalapeño pepper if available (if not use green)	

Roast bell peppers in broiler until blackened on all sides, turning often. Place in paper bag and let stand for 10 minutes. Peel, seed and quarter peppers and arrange on a platter. Heat half of olive oil (¼ cup) in a large cast iron or heavy skillet over medium heat. Add mushrooms and sauté until tender, season with salt and pepper to taste. Arrange on the platter with peppers. Pour the rest of the oil in the skillet and heat over medium-high heat. Sauté chopped jalapeño and garlic for 2

(continued)

23179-98

minutes. Add shrimp and sauté 3 minutes. Add parsley and stir. Spoon shrimp over mushrooms and peppers. Serves 8.

BAKED CLAMS
(Clams Casino)

1 dozen lg. fresh clams	Salt
4 T. finely chopped green pepper	6 slices bacon
4 T. finely chopped celery	1 c. fresh bread crumbs
2 T. chopped fresh parsley	¼ c. melted butter
Tabasco sauce	Rock salt

Shuck clams and chop clam meat. Save 12 half clam shells. Put about 1 inch of rock salt into a large shallow baking pan to provide a bed for clam half shells. Imbed the 12 reserved half shells in the rock salt leaving a ¼-inch border of shell out of the rock salt. Be very careful not to get any rock salt inside of shell. Place equal amounts of chopped clams into the 12 half shells. Put about 2 drops Tabasco sauce over each chopped clam. Place equal amounts of celery, onion, green pepper and parsley over chopped clam. Cover each clam with bread crumbs. Drizzle each with butter, cover with ½ strip of bacon. Preheat oven to 400° and bake until bacon is crisp, about 10 minutes.

CRAB DRESSING

1 lb. back fin crabmeat	8 c. fresh bread crumbs
½ c. minced onion	½ tsp. Worcestershire sauce
½ c. minced celery	¼ tsp. Tabasco sauce
½ tsp. salt	¼ c. chopped fresh parsley
2 tsp. Old Bay	4 eggs
¼ tsp. black pepper	Paprika

Combine eggs, parsley, Tabasco, Worcestershire, black pepper, Old Bay and salt and mix well. Feel through crabmeat and remove shells. Combine crabmeat with egg mixture and fold together. Pour dressing mixture into an ungreased baking dish and sprinkle with paprika. Bake uncovered in a 400° preheated oven for 20 minutes. The dressing should not be more than 2 inches thick in the baking dish. Add an additional 5 minutes of baking time for every inch over.

23179-98

SPAGHETTI WITH SEAFOOD SAUCE

¼ c. olive oil
1 tsp. fresh red chili pepper,
  chopped
6 garlic cloves, chopped
12 sea scallops
12 clams, scrubbed

8 mussels, scrubbed & debearded
4 c. fresh chopped tomatoes
  (plum)
8 lg. shrimp, (raw) peeled &
  deveined
12 oz. spaghetti
3 T. fresh chopped parsley

Heat oil in a large heavy skillet over medium heat. Combine garlic and chili pepper. Add clams and mussels. Cover and cook 10 minutes or until clams and mussels open. Add tomatoes, scallops and shrimp. Cook for 5 minutes, turning scallops and shrimp often. Cook pasta in large pot of boiling salted water until tender. Drain well. Add pasta to skillet and toss to coat with sauce. Transfer to large platter and garnish with parsley. Serves 4.

CRAB & CHICKEN ROLL UPS

2 T. minced onions
2 T. minced fresh parsley
1 c. grated Swiss cheese
8 oz. back fin crabmeat
1 tsp. minced fresh dill
1 tsp. minced garlic

4 boneless, skinless chicken
  breast halves
2 well beaten eggs
4 c. fresh bread crumbs
2 T. butter
2 T. peanut oil (if you have it)

Combine onion, parsley, dill, garlic, cheese and crab in a bowl and mix well. Place each chicken breast between 2 sheets of waxed paper, and flatten to ¼ inch thickness or thinner, using a mallet or rolling pin. Place ¼ mixture in center of flattened chicken breast and roll up while folding over end to seal. Sprinkle with black pepper. Dredge each roll up in egg and roll in bread crumbs. Melt butter and oil in large heavy skillet over medium heat. Place roll up in skillet, seam side down. Cook until golden brown; about 10 minutes on each side. Serve with Bearnaise sauce.

23179-98

POO BEAR CHICKEN

1 c. all-purpose flour
1 tsp. salt
1 tsp. paprika
¼ tsp. white pepper
1 (3-lb.) chicken, cut up into
  pieces

½ c. butter, melted
Vegetable spray
¼ c. butter, melted
¼ c. honey
¼ c. fresh lime juice
½ c. sweetened flaked coconut

Combine flour, salt, paprika and pepper in a plastic bag. Shake to mix. Place 2 pieces of chicken in bag. Shake well to coat chicken. Dip floured chicken in ½ cup melted butter. Place chicken, skin side up, in 9 x 13 x 2-inch baking dish coated with cooking spray. Repeat process with remaining flour mixture, chicken, and butter. Bake uncovered at 400° for for 30 minutes. Drain off pan drippings. Turn chicken over. Combine ¼ cup butter, honey, and lemon juice. Pour over chicken. Cover and bake 45 minutes, basting frequently with pan juices. Sprinkle coconut over chicken during last 15 minutes of baking. Makes 4 servings.

Melissa Cade
Daughter

TARRAGON & GARLIC GRILLED GAME HENS

4 game hens
4 cloves garlic, crushed &
  chopped
½ tsp. black pepper
½ tsp. salt

1 T. fresh chopped tarragon or 1
  tsp. dried
½ c. peanut oil
¼ c. vinegar

With kitchen shears butterfly game hens by cutting down the back (or have your butcher do it). Snip the breast bone on each side. Bird should lay out flat with skin side up. Combine garlic, salt, pepper, tarragon, oil and vinegar in a blender and blend on medium speed for 20 seconds. Baste both sides of birds with marinade and place in a plastic storage bag. Pour remaining marinade over birds. Refrigerate overnight. Prepare grill for medium hot heat. Place birds on grill skin side up. Baste often with leftover marinade. After 25 minutes cook skin side down for 10 minutes or until skin is crisp. Serve hot. Serves 4.

23179-98

LEMON BAKED CHICKEN

1 (3 to 4-lb.) chicken, quartered
2 T. fresh lemon juice
3 minced garlic cloves

2 T. minced fresh oregano
Salt & pepper

Preheat oven to 400°. Sprinkle both sides of chicken with lemon juice, garlic, and oregano. Sprinkle with salt and pepper. Arrange chicken skin side up in 9 x 13-inch baking dish. Bake 45 minutes and serve with pan juices. Makes 4 servings.

SUNFLOWER CHICKEN

4 skinned and boned chicken
    breast halves
1 (14-oz.) can coconut milk
1 (3.75-oz.) pack sunflower
    kernels, chopped

¼ c. minced fresh cilantro
2 T. fresh lime juice
16 (6-inch) wooden skewers

In a medium bowl, mix together the cilantro and coconut milk. Cut chicken into one inch strips the full length of the breast. Place chicken in coconut milk mixture. Cover and chill for 3 hours. Soak wooden skewers in water for 30 minutes. Remove chicken from marinade and thread onto skewers. Brush chicken with lime juice and roll in chopped sunflower kernels. Cook chicken on a medium high heat grill, turning often to prevent burning. Makes 4 servings.

FRIED CHICKEN

1 c. corn oil
1 fryer, cut up
1 egg
¼ c. canned milk
1 c. fine cracker crumbs
⅛ tsp. paprika
¼ tsp. rubbed sage

½ tsp. chopped fresh thyme
⅛ tsp. onion salt
1 T. chopped fresh parsley
⅛ tsp. celery salt
⅛ tsp. salt
¼ tsp. black pepper
1 c. flour

Combine egg and milk and beat until well blended. Combine cracker crumbs, flour, paprika, sage, thyme, onion salt, salt, parsley, celery salt and pepper and mix well. Heat large heavy frying pan over medium-high heat. Dip chicken pieces in egg wash and roll in crumb mixture. Place in hot frying pan and brown on all sides. Reduce heat to medium-

(continued)

23179-98

low, cover and cook until tender, about 25 minutes. Remove and drain on paper towels. Makes 4 to 6 servings.

FALL OFF THE BONE BARBECUED RIBS

1 baby back rib rack, cut into 2 (5 or 6) rib pieces
½ c. commercial barbecue sauce (I use Kraft or Bullseye)
4 T. bourbon (less 2 sips)
1 bay leaf

Mix together bourbon and barbecue sauce and set aside. Place ribs in a large pot and cover with water. Bring pot to a boil. Reduce heat and simmer for 30 minutes. Gently remove ribs from pot and baste with bourbon sauce. Place on hot grill and grill for 15 minutes turning and basting often.

STUFFED PORK CHOPS

6 boneless loin pork chops (about ¾-inch thick)
Crab dressing (1 recipe)
Hollandaise sauce

Have your butcher cut a pocket in each pork chop for stuffing. Preheat oven to 400°. Place some stuffing (as much as you can) in the pocket of the pork chops. Lay pork chops in a large lightly oiled baking dish. Using an ice cream scoop, place scoops of crab dressing around the pork chops. Bake in preheated oven for 20-25 minutes. Transfer to a warm serving dish and cover with Hollandaise sauce. Serve hot. Serves 6.

MEAT LOAF

½ tsp. garlic powder
½ tsp. black pepper
1 tsp. salt
2 tsp. Worcestershire sauce
2 eggs
2 T. fresh parsley
¼ c. milk
4 slices white bread
2 lbs. ground round

Combine garlic powder, pepper, salt, Worcestershire, eggs, parsley and milk and mix well. Place bread slices in food processor and process

(continued)

23179-98

into crumbs. Combine bread crumbs, milk and egg mixture and ground round; mix well using your hands. Place mixture into an ungreased loaf pan. Place in a 400° preheated oven and bake for 45 minutes. Drain juices from cooked Meat Loaf and turn onto cutting board. Slice ¾ to 1-inch thick. Best served with mashed potatoes, peas and brown gravy. Makes 4 to 6 servings.

RECIPE FAVORITES

23179-98

Breads
&
Rolls

Helpful Hints

- Over-ripe bananas can be peeled and frozen in a plastic container until it's time to bake bread or cake.

- When baking bread, a small dish of water in the oven will help keep the crust from getting too hard or brown.

- Use shortening, not margarine or oil, to grease pans, as margarine and oil absorb more readily into the dough or batter (especially bread).

- Use a metal ice tray divider to cut biscuits in a hurry. Press into the dough, and biscuits will separate at dividing lines when baked.

- To make self-rising flour, mix 4 cups flour, 2 teaspoons salt and 2 tablespoons baking powder, and store in a tightly covered container.

- Hot water kills yeast. One way to tell the correct temperature is to pour the water over your forearm. If you cannot feel either hot or cold, the temperature is just right.

- When in doubt, always sift flour before measuring.

- When baking in a glass pan, reduce the oven temperature by 25°.

- When baking bread, you get a finer texture if you use milk. Water makes a coarser bread.

- If your biscuits are dry it could be from too much handling, or the oven temperature may not have been hot enough.

- Nut breads are better if stored 24 hours before serving.

- To make bread crumbs, toast the heels of bread and chop in a blender or food processor.

- Cracked eggs should only be used in dishes that are thoroughly cooked; they may contain bacteria.

- The freshness of eggs can be tested by placing them in a large bowl of cold water; if they float, do not use them.

- For a quick, low-fat crunchy topping for muffins, sprinkle the tops with Grape-Nuts cereal before baking.

Breads & Rolls

CHEESE SPOON BREAD

3 c. milk	1 c. grated sharp cheddar cheese
1 T. sugar	2 T. butter
¾ tsp. salt	4 eggs, separated
¼ tsp. cayenne pepper	¼ tsp. black pepper
1 c. cornmeal	

Position rack in center of oven and preheat oven to 350°. Butter a 2-quart baking dish. Combine milk, sugar, salt and pepper in a medium saucepan and heat over medium heat until bubbles form around edges of pan. Gradually stir in cornmeal, stir and cook about 5 minutes until mixture is thick and creamy. Remove from heat. Add cheese and butter and mix until butter melts. Beat egg yolks well and stir into cornmeal mixture. Beat whites in large bowl until stiff but not dry. Mix ¼ of egg whites into cornmeal mixture. Gradually fold in remaining whites. Pour mixture into baking dish and bake for 55 minutes or until puffed, golden and knife inserted in center comes out clean. Serve hot. Makes 6 servings.

CHEF DIRT'S SPOON BREAD

½ c. warm unseasoned mashed	2 T. butter
potatoes	1 c. milk
1⅔ c. boiling water	2 lg. eggs, lightly beaten
1 c. cornmeal	2 tsp. baking powder
1 tsp. salt	

Pour water over cornmeal and mashed potatoes gradually, stirring until smooth. Add salt and butter, stirring until blended. Cool for 10 minutes. Gradually stir in milk and eggs. Add baking powder. Stir until blended. Pour mixture into a lightly greased 1½-quart baking dish. Bake at 375° for 40 minutes or until golden brown on top. Serves 4 to 6.

23179-98

HUSH PUPPIES

1 c. self-rising flour	2 T. minced onion
½ c. self-rising cornmeal	⅓ c. milk
1 egg, beaten well	½ tsp. Old Bay seasoning
¼ tsp. sugar	Corn oil
1 T. fresh chopped parsley	

Combine flour, cornmeal, egg, sugar, parsley, onion and Old Bay. Add milk and stir until all dry ingredients are wet. You should be able to form a wet, sticky ball using 2 spoons. If too dry add more milk, if too wet add more flour. Heat about 2 cups corn oil in a 2-quart saucepan (or 3 to 4 inches of oil in the pan) to 375°. Drop rounded tablespoonfuls of batter into hot oil and cook until golden brown. Drain on paper towels. Makes 15 to 20 golf ball-size Hush Puppies.

CORNBREAD

½ c. cornmeal (self-rising)	1 egg, beaten
½ c. flour (self-rising)	1 c. milk
½ tsp. salt	2 T. sour cream
2 T. corn oil + 1 T.	

Place a 10-inch cast iron frying pan in the oven and preheat oven to 425°. Combine cornmeal, flour, salt, sugar, 2 tablespoons oil, egg, milk and sour cream; stir until lumps disappear. Remove hot frying pan from oven, coat with 1 tablespoon of oil. Pour batter into frying pan. Return frying pan to oven and bake until golden brown on top, about 15 minutes. Cut into wedges and serve. Serves 4 to 6.

OUTER BANKS CORN MUFFINS

½ c. diced sweet red pepper	1½ c. blue cornmeal
¼ c. diced sweet bell pepper (green or yellow)	1 c. all-purpose flour
⅛ c. diced jalapeño pepper (seeds removed)	⅓ c. sugar
	1 T. baking powder
¼ c. chopped green onions	1 tsp. salt
¼ c. plus 2 T. butter	2 lg. eggs, lightly beaten
½ c. oil	1 c. milk
1 T. bacon fat	½ c. half-and-half
	1 c. chopped country ham

(continued)

23179-98

Sauté peppers and onion in bacon fat until tender; set aside. Combine butter and shortening in a small saucepan; melt over low heat, set aside to cool. Combine cornmeal, flour, sugar, baking powder and salt. Mix well and set aside. Combine eggs, milk, half-and-half and ham. Stir in sautéed vegetables and melted butter mixture. Add to dry ingredients (to include ham) stirring just until moistened. Spoon into greased and floured muffin pans, filling about three-fourths full. Bake at 350° for 20 to 30 minutes. Makes 24. **Note:** You may use yellow or white cornmeal instead of blue.

REFRIGERATOR ANGEL BISCUITS

2 pkgs. dry yeast
1 c. lukewarm water
1 T. sugar
1 tsp. salt
1 tsp. soda

¾ c. corn oil
2 c. buttermilk
5 c. self-rising flour (I use
  Southern Biscuit)

Dissolve yeast in lukewarm water, add sugar to water an stir until yeast dissolves. Add rest of ingredients and mix well. Pinch off amount needed and refrigerate rest. Shape biscuits and place in ungreased baking pan, touching each other. Bake at 425° until tops are golden brown. Will keep in refrigerator for 1 week.

FRIED CORNBREAD
(CORN CAKES)

1 egg, beaten
¾ c. self-rising flour
¼ c. self-rising cornmeal
¾ c. buttermilk
2 T. melted bacon fat or oil

½ tsp. salt
1 T. finely chopped jalapeño
  pepper (opt.)
1 T. finely chopped onion

Combine all ingredients and mix until lump free. Heat griddle or large skillet over medium heat and grease well with oil or fat. Pour about 6 tablespoons onto hot surface. When bubble form, flip over and cook other side until golden brown. Batter will thicken as it sets; thin with water as needed. Serves 4.

23179-98

CORN FRITTERS

2 c. vegetable oil	2 eggs, slightly beaten
1 c. self-rising flour	1 (16-oz.) can whole kernel corn,
1 tsp. salt	drained (reserve ¼ c. liquid)

Heat oil in medium-size saucepan to 375°. Combine flour, salt, eggs and reserved corn liquid. Mix well. Stir in corn. Drop by rounded tablespoonfuls into hot oil. Fry until golden brown. Drain on paper towels. Makes about 24.

PLAN AHEAD YEAST ROLLS

½ pkg. dry yeast	4½ T. shortening
¾ c. warm water	1 egg, slightly beaten
½ c. unseasoned lukewarm	3½ to 4 c. all-purpose flour
mashed potatoes (mash out all	¾ tsp. salt
lumps	
5 T. sugar	

Dissolve yeast in warm water in a large bowl. Stir in potatoes, sugar, shortening, eggs, salt and 1½ cups of the flour. Beat until smooth. Mix in enough remaining flour to make dough easy to handle. Place dough on lightly floured surface, knead until smooth and elastic. Place in greased bowl. Lightly coat the top of dough with oil. Cover bowl tightly; refrigerate at least 8 hours, but no longer than 5 days. When ready for use, remove from refrigerator, punch down, cut pieces to desired size. Place in lightly greased bread or muffin pans. Let rise in warm place until double in size (about 2 to 2½ hours). Bake in a 400° preheated oven until tops are golden brown (about 15 minutes).

BUTTERMILK PANCAKES

1 c. all-purpose flour (I use	1 egg, well beaten
Southern Biscuit)	2 T. oil
1 c. buttermilk	½ tsp. vanilla extract

Combine all ingredients and beat only until smooth. Grease hot griddle heated over medium-high heat. Pour 3 to 4 tablespoons batter onto hot griddle. Cook until puffed and dry around edges. Flip and cook other side until golden brown.

23179-98

Pies,
Pastry
&
Desserts

Helpful Hints

- Egg whites need to be at room temperature for greater volume when whipped. Remember this when making meringue.

- When preparing several batches of pie dough, roll dough out between sheets of plastic wrap. Stack the discs in a pizza box, and keep the box in the freezer. Next time you're making pie, pull out the required crusts.

- Place your pie plate on a cake stand when placing the pie dough in it and fluting the edges. The cake stand will make it easier to turn the pie plate, and you won't have to stoop over.

- Many kitchen utensils can be used to make decorative pie edges. For a scalloped edge, use a spoon. Crosshatched and herringbone patterns are achieved with a fork. For a sharply pointed effect, use a can opener to cut out points around the rim.

- Dipping strawberries in chocolate? Stick toothpicks into the stem end of the berry. Coat the berries with chocolate, shaking off any excess. Turn the berries upside down and stick the toothpick into a block of styrofoam until the chocolate is set. The finished berries will have chocolate with no flat spots. Another easy solution is to place dipped berries dipped-side up in the holes of an egg carton.

- Keep strawberries fresh for up to ten days by refrigerating them (unwashed) in an airtight container between layers of paper towels.

- When grating citrus peel, bits of peel are often stuck in the holes of the grater. Rather than waste the peel, you can easily brush it off by using a clean toothbrush.

- To core a pear, slice the pear in half lengthwise. Use a melon baller to cut out the central core, using a circular motion. Draw the melon baller to the top of the pear, removing the interior stem as you go.

- When cutting up dried fruit, it sometimes sticks to the blade of the knife. To prevent this problem, coat the blade of your knife with a thin film of vegetable spray before cutting.

- Cutting dessert bars is easier if you score the bars as soon as the pan comes out of the oven. When the bars cool, cut along the scored lines.

- When cutting butter into flour for pastry dough, the process is made easier if you cut the butter into small pieces before adding it to the flour.

Pies, Pastry & Desserts

TIPSY BREAD PUDDING

½ c. milk
1 c. raisins
⅓ c. Jim Beam bourbon (less 2 sips)
10 c. bread crumbs (made from day old bread)

1⅓ c. sugar
6 T. butter
4 lg. eggs
1 tsp. cinnamon
½ tsp. nutmeg
1⅓ c. chopped pecans

Put raisins in a small bowl and cover with bourbon; let set 1 hour. Preheat oven to 350°. Butter a 11 x 9 x 2-inch baking dish. Drain raisins and reserve liquid. Mix liquid with 4 ounces of Coke and pour over ice. Now drink liquid. Combine raisins, sugar, butter and cinnamon and nutmeg in a large bowl and mix well. Combine eggs and milk in blender and blend on high for 15 seconds. Add egg mixture to raisins mixture and mix well. Pour this mixture over bread crumbs, cover with aluminum foil and bake for 1 hour. Remove from oven and let cool for 20 minutes. Spoon pudding into bowls.

GRANNY'S BROWN BETTY

2 c. plain bread crumbs
2 lg. Granny Smith apples, cored, peeled & thinly sliced
⅓ c. firmly packed brown sugar
2 tsp. vanilla extract

1½ tsp. fresh lemon juice
½ tsp. lemon zest
¼ tsp. cinnamon
1 pinch nutmeg

Preheat oven to 450°. Spread bread crumbs in large baking pan and bake until starts to turn brown, about 5 minutes. Mix crumbs and butter in a bowl. Combine apples, sugar, vanilla, lemon juice, lemon zest, cinnamon and nutmeg in a large bowl; stir well. Spread ⅓ of bread crumb mixture over the bottom of a 6-cup baking dish. Spoon apple mixture over bread crumbs. Spread remaining bread crumbs over apples. Cover with aluminum foil. Bake in preheated oven for 35 minutes. Remove foil and bake another 10 minutes until bread crumbs brown. Let stand 30 minutes before serving. Serve with vanilla ice cream.

23179-98

CHEF "DIRT PUDDING" WITH DIRT-ETT CLEAN SAUCE

2 T. sugar
3 lg. eggs, lightly beaten
½ tsp. fresh ground nutmeg
2 T. brown sugar (dark)
10 Oreo cookies, broken up
¼ c. butter, melted
2¾ c. cream, whipping cream

About 4 cups cubed bread (use loaf bread that has not been sliced, French bread will do nicely, and cut into cubes about ½ inch square)
½ c. raisins

Smash cookie pieces real fine or put in food processor and process for about 15 to 20 seconds. Set aside. Combine eggs, sugar, brown sugar and nutmeg. Stir in butter and cream. Gently stir in bread and raisins. Pour half of mixture into a lightly greased 2-quart baking dish. Cover with two-thirds cookie crumbs. Add remainder of bread mixture and cover this layer with the remaining cookie crumbs. Bake at 375° for 55 minutes. Cover with aluminum foil after 30 minutes of baking time. Let stand for 10 minutes before serving. Serve hot with "Dirt-Ett Clean Sauce."

Dirt-Ett Clean Sauce:

⅓ c. sugar
3 T. light brown sugar
1 T. all-purpose flour
⅛ tsp. fresh ground nutmeg
⅛ tsp. fresh ground cinnamon
⅛ tsp. fresh grated ginger

2 T. butter, softened
1¼ c. cream (whipping cream will do)
1 T. vanilla extract (pure, do not use imitation)
1 lg. egg, well beaten

Mix sugar, brown sugar, flour, nutmeg, cinnamon, egg, butter, ginger and cream. Mix well and pour into a heavy saucepan; cook over medium heat, whisk constantly and cook for about 10 minutes or until thickened. Remove from heat and stir in vanilla. Serve warm over "Dirt Pudding."

BANANA NUT BREAD

1 c. sugar
½ c. shortening
2 eggs, well beaten
2 c. flour
1 tsp. salt

1 tsp. baking powder
1 tsp. soda
3 tsp. sour cream
3 bananas, mashed
1 c. chopped pecans

Mix together sugar and shortening until mixture resembles thick, heavy cream. Add eggs, sift in flour with salt, baking powder and soda.

(continued)

23179-98

Mix all ingredients well with electric mixer. Add sour cream, bananas and nuts and mix lightly. Pour mixture into buttered 5 x 10 x 3-inch loaf pan. Bake at 350° for 30 to 40 minutes. Serve warm slices with key lime orange sauce.

Terry "Banana Melon" Dancesia
Binghamton, NY

AMBROSIA

2 c. fresh pineapple, cut into chunks
½ c. green & red seedless grapes
½ c. fresh orange sections, seeds & membranes removed
½ c. fresh pink grapefruit sections, seeds & membranes removed

½ c. Peter Paul sweetened coconut flakes
½ c. sour cream
14 fresh peach halves, skin removed
½ c. coarse chopped pecans
½ c. grated mild cheddar cheese

Combine pineapple, grapes, orange, grapefruit and coconut. Chill for 2 hours in refrigerator. Toss; add sour cream. Mix well and spoon into peach halves. Top with cheddar cheese and pecans.

EASY FRUIT SORBET

1 c. fresh finely chopped peaches or mangos
Juice from ½ fresh lemon
½ c. water

1 c. sugar
½ c. dark rum
Key lime orange sauce (opt.)

Combine lemon juice, water, rum and sugar in 1-quart saucepan and bring to a boil stirring constantly. Remove pan from heat and let cool. Add fruit. Mix well. Pour mixture into sorbet cups or dessert cups (4). Freeze up to 8 hours, stirring 3 times during freezing. Top with key lime orange sauce if desired.

23179-98

WING NUT BROWNIES

2 (1-oz.) squares unsweetened
  chocolate
⅓ c. shortening
1 c. sugar
2 eggs

½ tsp. vanilla
¾ c. self-rising flour
¼ c. chopped pecans
¼ c. chopped walnuts

Heat oven to 350°. Heat chocolate and shortening in 2-quart sauce-pan over low heat, stirring constantly, until melted; remove from heat. Mix in sugar, eggs, and vanilla; stir in flour and nuts. Spread in a greased pan (use shortening), approximately 8 x 8 x 2-inch. Bake until brownies begin to pull away from sides of pan, 30 to 35 minutes. Cool slightly and cut into squares.

Cindy Swarmer
Grand Daughter

OUTER BANKS LIME PIE

8 lg. eggs, lightly beaten
2 c. sugar
⅔ c. fresh lime juice
2 T. lime zest
Dash salt

2 (9-inch) graham cracker crusts
1 c. unsalted butter, softened
2 c. whipping cream
¼ c. sifted powdered sugar
2 tsp. vanilla extract
Fresh grated nutmeg

Combine eggs, sugar, lime juice, lime zest and salt in top of double boiler; bring water to a boil. Reduce heat to low. Cook whisking con-stantly, until thickened. Add butter, cook, whisking constantly, until butter melts and mixture thickens. Pour into graham cracker crust. Bake in a 300° preheated oven for 20 minutes. Cover and chill eight hours. Beat whipping cream at high speed with an electric mixter until foamy. Gradu-ally add powdered sugar, beating until soft peaks form. Stir in vanilla and spread over chilled pies. Garnish lightly with fresh grated nutmeg. Chill for one hour and serve. **Note:** Nothing can take the place of fresh grated nutmeg. The flavor and aroma cannot be matched by the processed and canned nutmeg. The whole nutmeg keeps nicely in a small sealed jar and you can grate as needed. No kitchen should be without it. I know this pie will not be as good without it.

23179-98

SASSY PEACH PIE

1 c. sugar	¼ c. bourbon
½ tsp. lemon zest	2 tsp. fresh lemon juice
½ tsp. orange zest	2 T. cornstarch
4 c. fresh peaches	¼ c. light corn syrup
¼ tsp. nutmeg	1 pkg. pie crust mix
¼ tsp. cinnamon	

Combine first 10 ingredients in a 2-quart saucepan and simmer until peaches are tender and liquid is slightly thickened. Prepare pie crust as directed on package. Roll ⅔ of pastry to ⅛ inch thickness on a lightly floured surface. Lightly grease a 9-inch pie plate and dust with flour. Place the rolled out crust in the pie plate and form. Trim off excess pastry along the edges. Spoon filling into shell. Roll remaining pastry to ⅛ inch thickness and lay across pie plate and pinch together with bottom shell. Cut slits in top of pie crust (about 6). Dot with butter and bake in 425° oven for 35 to 40 minutes. Serve warm with vanilla ice cream or key lime sauce (warmed).

Stacey Swarmer
Granddaughter

AUNT VICTORIA'S APPLE PIE

For pie filling:

¾ c. sugar	6 c. thinly sliced pared apples
¼ c. all-purpose flour	(use a tart apple such as Granny
½ tsp. ground nutmeg (grind	Smith, McIntosh or Jonathan)
fresh if you can)	2 T. butter (country fresh if you
½ tsp. ground cinnamon (grind	can get it, if not the store bought
fresh if you can)	kind will do)
⅛ tsp. salt (or a dash)	

Mix sugar, flour, nutmeg, apples, cinnamon and salt; stir well and set aside.

Make pie crust:

1¾ c. all-purpose flour	1 tsp. salt
½ c. vegetable oil	3-4 T. cold water

Mix flour, oil and salt until particles are the size of a small pea. Sprinkle in water, one tablespoon at a time, mixing until all flour is moistened and pastry almost cleans side of bowl. (If pastry seems dry, 1 to 2 tablespoons of oil can be added.) Do not add additional water. Divide pastry in half. Roll each piece of pastry between waxed paper

(continued)

to fit a nine-inch pie plate. Roll bottom pastry 2 inches larger than pie plate. Lightly coat pie plate with shortening and dust with flour. Remove waxed paper from top of pie plate bottom crust, lay pastry in pie plate and form to bottom and sides. Trim off excess. Pour apple mixture into pie plate. Dot with butter. Remove top layer of waxed paper from top crust and place over top of pie plate. Pinch edges together to seal top with bottom pastry, cut slits in top pastry to allow steam to escape. Cover edge with 3 inch strip of aluminum foil; remove foil during last 15 minutes of baking. Place pie in a 425° preheated oven. Bake until crust is golden brown and juice begins to bubble through slits in crust, about 40 to 50 minutes. Allow to cool one hour before cutting. **Note:** Substitute peaches for apples, for a great peach pie.

Victoria Stevens
Great Aunt
Hurley, VA

FROGGY COBBLER

(Peach & Apple)

1 c. self-rising flour (I use
  Southern Biscuit)
2 sticks unsalted butter
3 c. fresh peaches, peel
  removed & sliced
1 c. Granny Smith apples, peel
  removed & sliced

Pinch of salt (⅛ tsp.)
½ tsp. cinnamon
¼ tsp. nutmeg
1 T. fresh lemon juice
2 c. sugar (divided)

Melt butter in 9 x 13-inch baking dish. Combine flour, 1 cup sugar, butter, and salt. Pour this batter into the baking dish. **Do not stir.** Combine 1 cup sugar, peach and apple slices and lemon juice in a 3-quart saucepan. Bring to a boil over high heat, stirring constantly. Remove from heat, add cinnamon and nutmeg, stir to mix slightly. Pour over the batter. **Do not stir.** Bake at 375° for 40 to 45 minutes or until golden brown. Serve warm with vanilla ice cream. Makes 8 to 10 servings.

Alexandria Cade
Granddaughter

23179-98

JELLY BEAN SALAD

1 c. assorted jelly beans
1 c. sliced bananas
1 T. lemon juice
½ c. grated dark sweet chocolate
¼ c. flaked sweetened coconut

½ c. pecan halves
½ c. honey
½ c. sm. white seedless grapes
½ pt. whipping cream

Place sliced bananas in large bowl; add lemon juice and toss. Add grapes, pecans, coconut, jelly beans and honey and toss. Spoon onto small salad plates. Prepare whipped cream and place dollops over each salad; garnish with grated chocolate (chocolate will grate easier if you place it in freezer for 5 minutes). Keep chilled until serving. Makes about 6 servings.

GRANDMA'S GINGERBREAD

½ c. butter
½ c. sugar
1 egg
1 c. molasses
2½ c. all-purpose flour, sifted
1½ tsp. soda

½ tsp. salt
1 tsp. ground cinnamon
1 tsp. ground cloves
1 tsp. ground ginger
1 c. hot water

Cream butter. Gradually add sugar, mixing at the same time. Add egg and molasses while mixing. Combine ginger, cloves, cinnamon, salt, soda and flour to the butter and egg mixture; alternate with hot water, beginning and ending with flour mixture. Beat well after each addition, making batter. Pour the batter into a lightly buttered and floured 9-inch pan. Bake in a 350° preheated oven until a toothpick inserted in the center comes out clean, about 35 to 40 minutes. Serve warm with lemon sauce.

23179-98

Recipe Favorites

Cakes,
Cookies
&
Candy

Helpful Hints

- Push animal shaped cookie cutters lightly into icing on cakes or cupcakes. Fill depressed outlines with chocolate icing or decorating confections.

- Fill flat bottomed ice cream cones half full with cake batter and bake. Top with icing and decorating confections.

- Marshmallows can be used for candle holders on cakes.

- To keep the cake plate clean while frosting, slide 6-inch strips of waxed paper under each side of the cake. Once the cake is frosted and the frosting is set, pull the strips away leaving a clean plate.

- When decorating a cake with chocolate, you can make a quick decorating tube. Put chocolate in a heat-safe zipper-lock plastic bag. Immerse in simmering water until the chocolate is melted. Snip off the tip of one corner, and you can squeeze the chocolate out of the bag.

- Professionally decorated cakes have a silky, molten look. To get that appearance, frost your cake as usual, then use a hair dryer to blow-dry the surface. The slight melting of the frosting will give it that lustrous appearance.

- To ensure that you have equal amounts of batter in each pan when making a layered cake, use a kitchen scale to measure the weight.

- To make cookie crumbs for your recipes, put cookies into a plastic bag and run a rolling pin back and forth until they are the right size.

- To decorate cookies with chocolate, place cookies on a rack over waxed paper. Dip the tines of a fork with chocolate, and wave the fork gently back and forth making wavy lines.

- A gadget that works well for decorating sugar cookies is an empty plastic thread spool. Simply press the spool into the dough, imprinting a pretty flower design.

- Some holiday cookies require an indent on top to fill with jam or chocolate. Use the rounded end of a honey dipper to make the indent.

- When a recipe calls for packed brown sugar, fill the correct size measuring cup with the sugar, and then use the next smaller size cup to pack the brown sugar into its cup.

Cakes, Cookies & Candy

PRALINE COOKIES

1½ c. packed dark brown sugar
1 egg
1 tsp. vanilla extract

1 c. coarsely chopped pecans
1½ c. sifted all-purpose flour
½ c. soft butter

Mix together butter, sugar and egg until creamy. Mix in rest of ingredients. Refrigerate until easy to handle. Preheat oven to 375°. Shape dough into 1-inch balls and place 3 inches apart on a greased cookie sheet. Cover the bottom of a large glass with a damp piece of cheese cloth and flatten balls to approximately ⅛ inch thick. Bake 13 minutes. Makes about 3 dozen cookies.

CRISPY TREATS
(Just For Kids)

⅓ c. butter
½ lb. marshmallows
½ tsp. vanilla

1 (5½-oz.) box of Rice Krispies
1 (16-oz.) jar chocolate fudge
topping

Combine butter and marshmallows in a double boiler and melt. Add vanilla. Beat thoroughly. Place Rice Krispies in a large bowl. Pour marshmallow mixture over Rice Krispies and stir well. Press into a buttered 2-quart baking dish or pan. Spread chocolate fudge topping on top of mixture. Refrigerate for 1 hour. Cut into squares and serve.

ANNE HARRISON COOKIES

1 c. (2 sticks) unsalted butter
(room temp.)
¾ c. sugar
¾ c. firmly packed golden brown
sugar
1 T. vanilla extract
1 T. Frangelico (hazelnut liqueur)
1 T. Royal Cream Kahlua

2 lg. eggs
2½ c. all-purpose flour
1 tsp. baking soda
½ tsp. salt
2 (11½-oz.) pkg. white chocolate
chips
2 c. chopped macadamia nuts

Preheat oven to 325°. Using electric mixer, beat butter, both sugars, vanilla extract, Frangelico and Royale Cream Kahlua in large bowl until

(continued)

23179-98

light and fluffy. Add eggs and beat well. Mix flour, baking soda and salt in small bowl. Stir into butter mixture. Mix in chocolate chips and macadamia nuts. Drop batter by ¼ cupfuls onto ungreased cookie sheets, spacing apart. Bake until cookies are golden brown, about 16 minutes. Transfer cookies to racks and cool.

Geraldine S. Quesenberry
Sister

RECIPE FAVORITES

This & That

Helpful Hints

- To refinish antiques or revitalize wood, use equal parts of linseed oil, white vinegar and turpentine. Rub into the furniture or wood with a soft cloth and lots of elbow grease.

- To stop the ants in your pantry, seal off cracks where they are entering with putty or petroleum jelly. Also, try sprinkling red pepper on floors and counter tops.

- To fix sticking sliding doors, windows and drawers, rub wax along their tracks.

- To make a simple polish for copper bottom cookware, mix equal parts of flour and salt with vinegar to create a paste. Store the paste in the refrigerator.

- Applying baking soda on a damp sponge will remove starch deposits from an iron. Make sure the iron is cold and unplugged.

- Remove stale odors in the wash by adding baking soda.

- To clean Teflon™, combine 1 cup water, 2 tablespoons baking soda and ½ cup liquid bleach. Boil in stained pan for 5 to 10 minutes or until the stain disappears. Wash, rinse, dry and condition with oil before using the pan again.

- Corning Ware can be cleaned by filling it with water and dropping in two denture cleaning tablets. Let stand for 30 to 45 minutes.

- A little instant coffee will work wonders on your wood furniture. Just make a thick paste from instant coffee and a little water, and rub it into the nicks and scratches on your dark wood furniture. You'll be amazed at how new and beautiful those pieces will look.

- For a clogged shower head, boil it for 15 minutes in a mixture of ½ cup vinegar and 1 quart water.

- For a spicy aroma, toss dried orange or lemon rinds into the fireplace.

- Tin coffee cans make excellent freezer containers for cookies.

- Add raw rice to the salt shaker to keep the salt free-flowing.

- Ice cubes will help sharpen garbage disposal blades.

This & That

EGGS IN A BASKET
(For Little Kids & Big Ones Too)

1 slice bread   Melted butter
1 egg

Heat nonstick griddle or frying pan over medium heat. Brush both sides of bread slice with melted butter, using a 2¾-inch biscuit cutter (an assortment of tin cans with both ends removed makes great biscuit cutters) cut out the center of bread slice. Place bread slice in center of griddle. Break egg and pour into cut out in bread slice. After egg whites set on bottom, about 1 minute, flip over and fry the other side for 1 minute or until yolk is cooked to your liking. Flip over the cut out and toast the other side. Serves 1 child or ½ adult. Spoon Hollandaise sauce over egg for adult taste.

HUSH PUPPY CORN DOGS

1 c. yellow cornmeal   ¾ c. milk
½ c. all-purpose flour   10 all-beef hot dogs (I use
1½ tsp. baking powder   Hormel)
2 tsp. sugar   Vegetable oil
1 tsp. salt   10 (6-inch) wooden skewers
¼ tsp. onion powder   (soaked in water for 1 hour)
1 lg. egg, beaten

Combine first 6 ingredients in a large bowl; make a well in center. Combine egg and milk. Add to cornmeal mixture, stirring just until dry ingredients are moistened. Insert wooden skewer in one end of each hot dog, leaving a 2 to 3 inch handle. Dip each into batter coating completely. Pour oil to depth of 5 inches or more into a large heavy saucepan. Heat oil to about 375°. Fry dogs until golden brown, about 2 to 3 minutes. Drain on paper towels. Serve with ketchup and mustard.

Anna Rebecca Cade
Granddaughter

SALSA

5 fresh tomatoes, skinned,
seeded & chopped
3 sm. green onions with tops,
chopped
2 cloves garlic, crushed &
chopped

3 tsp. apple cider vinegar
1 T. chopped cilantro
½ tsp. sugar
1 T. chopped coriander
½ tsp. chili powder
1 tsp. chopped Habanero pepper

Combine all ingredients; toss to mix well. Chill for 4 hours. Serve. Makes about ¾ cup and is very hot.

FRESH ITALIAN DRESSING

1 c. olive oil
¼ c. lemon juice
¼ c. white vinegar
1 tsp. salt
1 tsp. sugar
½ tsp. dry mustard

½ tsp. paprika
1 T. fresh chopped oregano
1 tsp. fresh chopped thyme
2 garlic cloves, crushed &
chopped

Combine all ingredients in a blender. Blend on high for 10 seconds. Refrigerate up to 3 hours. Shake well and serve. Makes 1½ cups.

FRESH FRENCH DRESSING

1 c. olive oil
¼ c. vinegar
¼ c. fresh lemon juice
1 tsp. salt

½ tsp. dry mustard
½ tsp. fresh chopped chard or 1
tsp. parsley

Mix all ingredients well. Refrigerate up to 3 hours. Shake well and serve. Makes 1½ cups.

23179-98

FRESH THOUSAND ISLAND DRESSING

½ c. mayonnaise
¼ tsp. chili powder
1 T. chopped stuffed olives
1 tsp. chopped fresh chives
1 hard-boiled egg, chopped

¼ tsp. paprika
¼ tsp. white pepper
¼ tsp. salt
3 T. heavy cream

Mix all ingredients well. Chill up to 3 hours. Stir and serve. Makes ¾ cup.

FRESH BLUE CHEESE DRESSING

¾ c. crumbled blue cheese
4 oz. softened cream cheese

½ c. mayonnaise
⅓ c. heavy cream

Reserve ⅓ of blue cheese. Beat ½ cup blue cheese and cream cheese until well blended. Add mayonnaise and cream; beat until well blended and creamy. Stir in reserved blue cheese. Mix well. Chill up to 3 hours and serve. Makes 1½ cups.

HOLLANDAISE SAUCE

3 egg yolks
2 T. fresh lemon juice

1 stick butter (¼ lb.), softened
¼ tsp. salt

Combine egg yolks and lemon juice in top pan of double boiler. Beat with a wire whisk until blended. Add ⅓ of butter. Bring water to a boil in bottom part of double broiler. Place pot containing egg mixture over boiling water (water in bottom pan should not touch top pan when brought to a boil). Bring water to a boil. Reduce heat to low; cook, stirring constantly with wire whip, until butter melts. Add remaining butter, stir constantly until butter begins to melt. Add remaining butter, stirring constantly until melted. Cook, stirring constantly, 2 to 3 minutes or until smooth and thickened. Remove from heat and stir in salt. Serve over eggs, seafood and vegetables. Makes ⅔ to ¾ cup.

23179-98

BEARNAISE SAUCE

½ c. dry white wine
4 T. white vinegar
2 tsp. tarragon (fresh)

2 shallots, chopped fine
1 T. chopped fresh parsley
1 c. softened butter

Heat white wine, vinegar and shallots in a small saucepan. Cook until reduced by half. Lower the heat, add the parsley and tarragon. With a wire whisk, beat in the softened butter small amounts at a time until sauce is the thickness of Hollandaise. Serve over seafood or vegetables.

ROASTED GARLIC SAUCE

2 bulbs (heads) garlic, unpeeled
1 tsp. olive oil
1½ T. butter

1½ T. all-purpose flour
⅔ c. shrimp or chicken broth
2 tsp. minced fresh parsley

Place garlic on a piece of aluminum foil, and drizzle with olive oil. Fold and seal. Bake at 425° for 30 minutes and let cool. Melt butter in heavy saucepan over medium high heat. Cut the top off each garlic head and squeeze cooked garlic into a pan. Add flour, and cook, stirring constantly with a wire whisk while cooking over medium heat (about one minute). Add broth and parsley. Continue cooking, stirring constantly, until mixture is thick and bubbly. Makes about ⅔ cup. Serve over pasta or use to make seafood pizza.

CUCUMBER DILL SAUCE

1 c. sour cream
½ c. grated, seeded, peeled
cucumber (drained)

2 T. finely chopped shallot
1 T. chopped fresh dill

Mix all ingredients in a bowl. Season with a pinch of salt and pepper. Mix well, cover and chill for 6 hours. Serve over baked, broiled or grilled fish.

23179-98

KEY LIME ORANGE SAUCE

3 lg. oranges	1 cinnamon stick
1 tsp. key lime juice	3 T. chopped crystallized ginger
6 T. + 1 tsp. sugar	1 c. + 2 T. orange juice

Peel oranges and remove all white pith. Remove orange segments from membranes. Place segments in a medium bowl. Add orange juice. Place orange juice in a medium saucepan. Add sugar and cinnamon. Cook over low heat, stirring until sugar dissolves. Raise heat to medium and simmer until juice has reduced to about 6 tablespoons and is syrupy. Pour over oranges. Add ginger and let cool.

CAPER SAUCE

1 T. drained capers	1 c. seeded & chopped fresh
1 T. fresh lemon juice	tomatoes
1 tsp. fresh lime juice	¼ c. fresh chopped basil
1 chopped shallot	½ c. fresh chopped Italian parsley
½ c. olive oil	

Combine all ingredients in food processor and pulse about 6 times to blend well. Makes about ¾ cup. Serve over grilled fish or baked chicken.

GUACAMOLE

1 avocado, peeled, pit removed &	¼ tsp. white pepper
mashed	1 sm. onion, grated
1 garlic clove crushed & chopped	½ tsp. coriander
1 T. lemon juice	1 T. fresh chopped cilantro
1 tsp. salt	

Combine all ingredients in a food processor and process about 30 seconds. Stop every 5 seconds and scrape down from sides. Serve with raw vegetables for dipping.

23179-98

LEMON SAUCE

½ c. fresh squeezed lemon juice
2 tsp. lemon zest
2 T. sugar

2 tsp. cornstarch
¼ c. water
½ tsp. cream of tartar (opt.)

Put cornstarch in small saucepan. Gradually add water while stirring to dissolve cornstarch. Add all other ingredients and heat over medium heat until thickened. Stir continuously while heating. Serve hot over bread pudding, gingerbread or banana nut bread. Makes about ¾ cup.

BROWN GRAVY
(For Meat Loaf & Roast Beef)

1 (14½-oz.) can beef broth
1½ T. roux

Salt & pepper to taste
1 tsp. Worcestershire sauce

Combine beef broth, roux, pinch of salt, pinch of pepper and Worcestershire in a 1-quart saucepan over medium heat. Stirring constantly, bring mixture to a slow boil. Remove from heat, continue to stir for 1 minute and serve. Makes about 1½ cups. **Chicken Broth:** Use canned chicken broth to make chicken gravy.

TEMPURA BATTER
(For Frying Vegetables, Meat & Seafood)

8 oz. all-purpose flour
1 T. cornstarch
¼ tsp. salt
1 c. chilled water

1 egg yolk
2 egg whites, stiffly beaten
Corn or vegetable oil

Mix together the flour, cornstarch and salt in a medium size bowl. Make a well in the center. Mix water and egg yolk together and pour into the well. Stir in the flour and lightly blend. Fold in egg whites. Heat oil to 350°. Dip vegetables and meat in batter and deep fry in hot oil. Drain on paper towels.

(continued)

23179-98

Sauce:

1 inch fresh gingerroot, peeled and grated	1 tsp. grated fresh horseradish
2 T. grated turnip	¼ c. prepared mustard
	¼ c. soy sauce

Mix all ingredients together and keep covered.

GINGER PICKLES

1 c. white vinegar	2 T. finely chopped fresh ginger
½ c. sugar	3 c. thinly sliced cucumbers

Heat vinegar, sugar and ginger over low heat just until sugar has dissolved. Let cool to room temperature. Pour over sliced cucumber slices; cover and place in refrigerator. Marinate in refrigerator 6 hours before using.

ROUX
(Rooh)

Roux will be needed in some of the recipes in this book and is a must for a southern cook. It is used to thicken and give body to sauce, gravies, Creoles and jumbalias. There is no substitute. Make it up and store in refrigerator in an airtight container. Use as needed.

1½ c. all-purpose flour	¾ c. vegetable oil or bacon fat

Heat oil in 1-quart saucepan over medium heat. Cook until mixture is bubbly. Remove from heat, let cool and store in refrigerator. Use 1 tablespoon per 1 cup liquid.

FRIED ONION RINGS

3 lg. Vidalia or Spanish onions	1 T. cornstarch
½ c. milk	½ tsp. salt
1 egg	Corn oil
¾ c. all-purpose flour	

Cut onions into ¼ to ⅜ inch slices and separate into rings. Marinate onion rings in milk for 1 hour. Remove onion rings from milk and gently

(continued)

23179-98

blot with paper towels. Pour milk back into measuring cup and add enough milk to bring back to ½ cup. Add to egg, flour, cornstarch and salt. Mix all ingredients until smooth. Heat 3 to 4 inches corn oil in 2-quart saucepan to 375°. Dip each onion ring in batter, let excess drip back into bowl. Drop battered onion rings, 1 at a time, into hot oil. Fry no more than 6 at a time until golden brown (2 to 3 minutes), turning once. Drain on paper towels. Makes 4 to 5 servings.

S.O.S.

If you are over 50 years old and were in the army, you will remember this and know what S.O.S. means.

1 lb. hamburger (ground round)	**1 garlic clove, crushed**
2 c. milk	**2 T. roux**
¼ tsp. black pepper	**Toast**

Brown hamburger with garlic and drain. Add roux, milk, salt and pepper and simmer over medium-low heat stirring continually as it thickens. Serve over toast. Will serve 2 to 40 (depends who you ask).

SHRIMP STOCK

When you peel raw shrimp, always save the shells. Put them in a Ziploc bag and store in freezer.

4 c. water	**½ tsp. salt**
1 c. shrimp shells	

Combine water, shells and salt in a 2-quart saucepan. Bring to a boil, remove from heat. Let steep for 5 minutes. Drain and discard shells. Use in recipes instead of water, such as rice and fresh vegetables.

23179-98

INDEX OF RECIPES

POO BEAR CHICKEN	43	**Cakes, Cookies & Candy**	
RECOMMENDED MARINADES			
FOR BAKING, GRILLING OR		ANNE HARRISON COOKIES	59
BROILING FISH	27	CRISPY TREATS	59
ROCK ISLAND RED SNAPPER	35	PRALINE COOKIES	59
SCALLOPS WITH SPARKLING			
WINE & SAFFRON	40	**This & That**	
SEAFOOD LASAGNA	39		
SHRIMP AND SEASHELL		BEARNAISE SAUCE	64
PASTA WITH WINE AND		BROWN GRAVY	66
CREAM SAUCE	38	CAPER SAUCE	65
SPAGHETTI WITH SEAFOOD		CUCUMBER DILL SAUCE	64
SAUCE	42	EGGS IN A BASKET	61
STEAMED MUSSELS	31	FRESH BLUE CHEESE	
STUFFED PORK CHOPS	45	DRESSING	63
SUNFLOWER CHICKEN	44	FRESH FRENCH DRESSING	62
TARRAGON & GARLIC		FRESH ITALIAN DRESSING	62
GRILLED GAME HENS	43	FRESH THOUSAND ISLAND	
TUNA BURGERS	39	DRESSING	63
TUNA REBECCA	30	FRIED ONION RINGS	67
TUNA SAUSAGE	30	GINGER PICKLES	67
WHITE CLAM SAUCE OVER		GUACAMOLE	65
PASTA	36	HOLLANDAISE SAUCE	63
		HUSH PUPPY CORN DOGS	61
		KEY LIME ORANGE SAUCE	65
Breads & Rolls		LEMON SAUCE	66
		ROASTED GARLIC SAUCE	64
BUTTERMILK PANCAKES	50	ROUX	67
CHEESE SPOON BREAD	47	SALSA	62
CHEF DIRT'S SPOON BREAD	47	SHRIMP STOCK	68
CORN FRITTERS	50	S.O.S.	68
CORNBREAD	48	TEMPURA BATTER	66
FRIED CORNBREAD	49		
HUSH PUPPIES	48		
OUTER BANKS CORN			
MUFFINS	48		
PLAN AHEAD YEAST ROLLS	50		
REFRIGERATOR ANGEL			
BISCUITS	49		

Pies, Pastry & Desserts

AMBROSIA	53
AUNT VICTORIA'S APPLE PIE	55
BANANA NUT BREAD	52
CHEF "DIRT PUDDING" WITH	
DIRT-ETT CLEAN SAUCE	52
EASY FRUIT SORBET	53
FROGGY COBBLER	56
GRANDMA'S GINGERBREAD	57
GRANNY'S BROWN BETTY	51
JELLY BEAN SALAD	57
OUTER BANKS LIME PIE	54
SASSY PEACH PIE	55
TIPSY BREAD PUDDING	51
WING NUT BROWNIES	54

How to Order

Get your additional copies of this cookbook by returning an order form and your check or money order to:

Jerry G. Smith
P.O. Box 262
Harbinger, N.C. 27941
(252) 491-2403

Please send me _____ copies of the **Seafood and Things From The Outer Banks** cookbook at **$8.95** per copy and **$2.50** for shipping and handling per book. Enclosed is my check or money order for $_____.

Mail Books To:

Name_____

Address _____

City _____ State _____ Zip _____

✂ -

Please send me _____ copies of the **Seafood and Things From The Outer Banks** cookbook at **$8.95** per copy and **$2.50** for shipping and handling per book. Enclosed is my check or money order for $_____.

Mail Books To:

Name_____

Address _____

City _____ State _____ Zip _____

23179 j

Cooking Tips

1. After stewing a chicken, cool in broth before cutting into chunks; it will have twice the flavor.

2. To slice meat into thin strips, as for stir-fry dishes, partially freeze it so it will slice more easily.

3. A roast with the bone in will cook faster than a boneless roast. The bone carries the heat to the inside more quickly.

4. When making a roast, place dry onion soup mix in the bottom of your roaster pan. After removing the roast, add 1 can of mushroom soup and you will have a good brown gravy.

5. For a juicier hamburger, add cold water to the beef before grilling (1/2 cup to 1 pound of meat).

6. To freeze meatballs, place them on a cookie sheet until frozen. Place in plastic bags. They will stay separated so that you may remove as many as you want.

7. To keep cauliflower white while cooking, add a little milk to the water.

8. When boiling corn, add sugar to the water instead of salt. Salt will toughen the corn.

9. To ripen tomatoes, put them in a brown paper bag in a dark pantry, and they will ripen overnight.

10. To keep celery crisp, stand it upright in a pitcher of cold, salted water and refrigerate.

11. When cooking cabbage, place a small tin cup or can half full of vinegar on the stove near the cabbage. It will absorb the odor.

12. Potatoes soaked in salt water for 20 minutes before baking will bake more rapidly.

13. Let raw potatoes stand in cold water for at least a half-hour before frying in order to improve the crispness of French-fried potatoes. Dry potatoes thoroughly before adding to oil.

14. Use greased muffin tins as molds when baking stuffed green peppers.

15. A few drops of lemon juice in the water will whiten boiled potatoes.

16. Buy mushrooms before they "open." When stems and caps are attached firmly, mushrooms are truly fresh.

17. Do not use metal bowls when mixing salads. Use wood, glass or china.

18. Lettuce keeps better if you store it in the refrigerator without washing it. Keep the leaves dry. Wash lettuce the day you are going to use it.

19. Do not use soda to keep vegetables green. It destroys Vitamin C.

20. Do not despair if you oversalt gravy. Stir in some instant mashed potatoes to repair the damage. Just add a little more liquid in order to offset the thickening.

Herbs & Spices

Acquaint yourself with herbs and spices. Add in small amounts, ¼ teaspoon for every 4 servings. Crush dried herbs or snip fresh ones before using. Use 3 times more fresh herbs if substituting fresh for dried.

Basil Sweet, warm flavor with an aromatic odor. Use whole or ground. Good with lamb, fish, roast, stews, ground beef, vegetables, dressing and omelets.

Bay Leaves Pungent flavor. Use whole leaf but remove before serving. Good in vegetable dishes, seafood, stews and pickles.

Caraway Spicy taste and aromatic smell. Use in cakes, breads, soups, cheese and sauerkraut.

Chives Sweet, mild flavor like that of onion. Excellent in salads, fish, soups and potatoes.

Cilantro Use fresh. Excellent in salads, fish, chicken, rice, beans and Mexican dishes.

Curry Powder Spices are combined to proper proportions to give a distinct flavor to meat, poultry, fish and vegetables.

Dill Both seeds and leaves are flavorful. Leaves may be used as a garnish or cooked with fish, soup, dressings, potatoes and beans. Leaves or the whole plant may be used to flavor pickles.

Fennel Sweet, hot flavor. Both seeds and leaves are used. Use in small quantities in pies and baked goods. Leaves can be boiled with fish.

Ginger A pungent root, this aromatic spice is sold fresh, dried or ground. Use in pickles, preserves, cakes, cookies, soups and meat dishes.

Herbs & Spices

Marjoram May be used both dried or green. Use to flavor fish, poultry, omelets, lamb, stew, stuffing and tomato juice.

Mint Aromatic with a cool flavor. Excellent in beverages, fish, lamb, cheese, soup, peas, carrots, and fruit desserts.

Oregano Strong, aromatic odor. Use whole or ground in tomato juice, fish, eggs, pizza, omelets, chili, stew, gravy, poultry and vegetables.

Paprika A bright red pepper, this spice is used in meat, vegetables and soups or as a garnish for potatoes, salads or eggs.

Parsley Best when used fresh, but can be used dried as a garnish or as a seasoning. Try in fish, omelets, soup, meat, stuffing and mixed greens.

Rosemary Very aromatic. Can be used fresh or dried. Season fish, stuffing, beef, lamb, poultry, onions, eggs, bread and potatoes. Great in dressings.

Saffron Orange-yellow in color, this spice flavors or colors foods. Use in soup, chicken, rice and breads.

Sage Use fresh or dried. The flowers are sometimes used in salads. May be used in tomato juice, fish, omelets, beef, poultry, stuffing, cheese spreads and breads.

Tarragon Leaves have a pungent, hot taste. Use to flavor sauces, salads, fish, poultry, tomatoes, eggs, green beans, carrots and dressings.

Thyme Sprinkle leaves on fish or poultry before broiling or baking. Throw a few sprigs directly on coals shortly before meat is finished grilling.

Baking Breads

Hints for Baking Breads

1. Kneading dough for 30 seconds after mixing improves the texture of baking powder biscuits.

2. Instead of shortening, use cooking or salad oil in waffles and hot cakes.

3. When bread is baking, a small dish of water in the oven will help keep the crust from hardening.

4. Dip a spoon in hot water to measure shortening, butter, etc., and the fat will slip out more easily.

5. Small amounts of leftover corn may be added to pancake batter for variety.

6. To make bread crumbs, use the fine cutter of a food grinder and tie a large paper bag over the spout in order to prevent flying crumbs.

7. When you are doing any sort of baking, you get better results if you remember to preheat your cookie sheet, muffin tins or cake pans.

Rules for Use of Leavening Agents

1. In simple flour mixtures, use 2 teaspoons baking powder to leaven 1 cup flour. Reduce this amount 1/2 teaspoon for each egg used.

2. To 1 teaspoon soda use 2 1/4 teaspoons cream of tartar, 2 cups freshly soured milk, or 1 cup molasses.

3. To substitute soda and an acid for baking powder, divide the amount of baking powder by 4. Take that as your measure and add acid according to rule 2.

Proportions of Baking Powder to Flour

biscuits ....to 1 cup flour use 1 1/4 tsp. baking powder
cake with oil ....to 1 cup flour use 1 tsp. baking powder
muffins ....to 1 cup flour use 1 1/2 tsp. baking powder
popovers ....to 1 cup flour use 1 1/4 tsp. baking powder
waffles ....to 1 cup flour use 1 1/4 tsp. baking powder

Proportions of Liquid to Flour

drop batter ....to 1 cup liquid use 2 to 2 1/2 cups flour
pour batter ....to 1 cup liquid use 1 cup flour
soft dough ....to 1 cup liquid use 3 to 3 1/2 cups flour
stiff dough ....to 1 cup liquid use 4 cups flour

Time and Temperature Chart

Breads	Minutes	Temperature
biscuits	12 - 15	400° - 450°
cornbread	25 - 30	400° - 425°
gingerbread	40 - 50	350° - 370°
loaf	50 - 60	350° - 400°
nut bread	50 - 75	350°
popovers	30 - 40	425° - 450°
rolls	20 - 30	400° - 450°

Baking Desserts

Perfect Cookies

Cookie dough that is to be rolled is much easier to handle after it has been refrigerated for 10 to 30 minutes. This keeps the dough from sticking, even though it may be soft. If not done, the soft dough may require more flour and too much flour makes cookies hard and brittle. Place on a floured board only as much dough as can be easily managed. Flour the rolling pin slightly and roll lightly to desired thickness. Cut shapes close together and add trimmings to dough that needs to be rolled. Place pans or sheets in upper third of oven. Watch cookies carefully while baking in order to avoid burned edges. When sprinkling sugar on cookies, try putting it into a salt shaker in order to save time.

Perfect Pies

1. Pie crust will be better and easier to make if all the ingredients are cool.

2. The lower crust should be placed in the pan so that it covers the surface smoothly. Air pockets beneath the surface will push the crust out of shape while baking.

3. Folding the top crust over the lower crust before crimping will keep juices in the pie.

4. In making custard pie, bake at a high temperature for about ten minutes to prevent a soggy crust. Then finish baking at a low temperature.

5. When making cream pie, sprinkle crust with powdered sugar in order to prevent it from becoming soggy.

Perfect Cakes

1. Fill cake pans two-thirds full and spread batter into corners and sides, leaving a slight hollow in the center.

2. Cake is done when it shrinks from the sides of the pan or if it springs back when touched lightly with the finger.

3. After removing a cake from the oven, place it on a rack for about five minutes. Then, the sides should be loosened and the cake turned out on a rack in order to finish cooling.

4. Do not frost cakes until thoroughly cool.

5. Icing will remain where you put it if you sprinkle cake with powdered sugar first.

Time and Temperature Chart

Dessert	Time	Temperature
butter cake, layer	20-40 min.	380° - 400°
butter cake, loaf	40-60 min.	360° - 400°
cake, angel	50-60 min.	300° - 360°
cake, fruit	3-4 hrs.	275° - 325°
cake, sponge	40-60 min.	300° - 350°
cookies, molasses	18-20 min.	350° - 375°
cookies, thin	10-12 min.	380° - 390°
cream puffs	45-60 min.	300° - 350°
meringue	40-60 min.	250° - 300°
pie crust	20-40 min.	400° - 500°

Vegetables & Fruits

Vegetable	Cooking Method	Time
artichokes	boiled	40 min.
	steamed	45-60 min.
asparagus tips	boiled	10-15 min.
beans, lima	boiled	20-40 min.
	steamed	60 min.
beans, string	boiled	15-35 min.
	steamed	60 min.
beets, old	boiled or steamed	1-2 hours
beets, young with skin	boiled	30 min.
	steamed	60 min.
	baked	70-90 min.
broccoli, flowerets	boiled	5-10 min.
broccoli, stems	boiled	20-30 min.
brussels sprouts	boiled	20-30 min.
cabbage, chopped	boiled	10-20 min.
	steamed	25 min.
carrots, cut across	boiled	8-10 min.
	steamed	40 min.
cauliflower, flowerets	boiled	8-10 min.
cauliflower, stem down	boiled	20-30 min.
corn, green, tender	boiled	5-10 min.
	steamed	15 min.
	baked	20 min.
corn on the cob	boiled	8-10 min.
	steamed	15 min.
eggplant, whole	boiled	30 min.
	steamed	40 min.
	baked	45 min.
parsnips	boiled	25-40 min.
	steamed	60 min.
	baked	60-75 min.
peas, green	boiled or steamed	5-15 min.
potatoes	boiled	20-40 min.
	steamed	60 min.
	baked	45-60 min.
pumpkin or squash	boiled	20-40 min.
	steamed	45 min.
	baked	60 min.
tomatoes	boiled	5-15 min.
turnips	boiled	25-40 min.

Drying Time Table

Fruit	Sugar or Honey	Cooking Time
apricots	¼ c. for each cup of fruit	about 40 min.
figs	1 T. for each cup of fruit	about 30 min.
peaches	¼ c. for each cup of fruit	about 45 min.
prunes	2 T. for each cup of fruit	about 45 min.

Vegetables & Fruits

Buying Fresh Vegetables

Artichokes: Look for compact, tightly closed heads with green, clean-looking leaves. Avoid those with leaves that are brown or separated.

Asparagus: Stalks should be tender and firm; tips should be close and compact. Choose the stalks with very little white; they are more tender. Use asparagus soon because it toughens rapidly.

Beans, Snap: Those with small seeds inside the pods are best. Avoid beans with dry-looking pods.

Broccoli, Brussels Sprouts and Cauliflower: Flower clusters on broccoli and cauliflower should be tight and close together. Brussels sprouts should be firm and compact. Smudgy, dirty spots may indicate pests or disease.

Cabbage and Head Lettuce: Choose heads that are heavy for their size. Avoid cabbage with worm holes and lettuce with discoloration or soft rot.

Cucumbers: Choose long, slender cucumbers for best quality. May be dark or medium green, but yellow ones are undesirable.

Mushrooms: Caps should be closed around the stems. Avoid black or brown gills.

Peas and Lima Beans: Select pods that are well-filled but not bulging. Avoid dried, spotted, yellow, or flabby pods.

Buying Fresh Fruits

Bananas: Skin should be free of bruises and black or brown spots. Purchase them green and allow them to ripen at home at room temperature.

Berries: Select plump, solid berries with good color. Avoid stained containers which indicate wet or leaky berries. Berries with clinging caps, such as blackberries and raspberries, may be unripe. Strawberries without caps may be overripe.

Melons: In cantaloupes, thick, close netting on the rind indicates best quality. Cantaloupes are ripe when the stem scar is smooth and the space between the netting is yellow or yellow-green. They are best when fully ripe with fruity odor.

Honeydews are ripe when rind has creamy to yellowish color and velvety texture. Immature honeydews are whitish-green.

Ripe watermelons have some yellow color on one side. If melons are white or pale green on one side, they are not ripe.

Oranges, Grapefruit and Lemons: Choose those heavy for their size. Smoother, thinner skins usually indicate more juice. Most skin markings do not affect quality. Oranges with a slight greenish tinge may be just as ripe as fully colored ones. Light or greenish-yellow lemons are more tart than deep yellow ones. Avoid citrus fruits showing withered, sunken or soft areas.

Napkin Folding

General Tips:
Use well-starched linen napkins if possible. For more complicated folds, 24-inch napkins work best. Practice the folds with newspapers. Children can help. Once they learn the folds, they will have fun!

Shield

Easy fold. Elegant with monogram in corner.

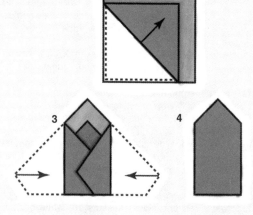

Instructions:
1. Fold into quarter size. If monogrammed, ornate corner should face down.
2. Turn up folded corner three-quarters.
3. Overlap right side and left side points.
4. Turn over; adjust sides so that they are even, single point in center.
5. Place point up or down on plate, or left of plate.

Rosette

Elegant on plate.

Instructions:
1. Fold left and right edges to center, leaving ½" opening along center.
2. Pleat firmly from top edge to bottom edge. Sharpen edges with hot iron.
3. Pinch center together. If necessary, use small piece of pipe cleaner to secure and top with single flower.
4. Spread out rosette.

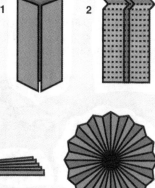

Napkin Folding

Candle

Easy to do; can be decorated.

Instructions:
1. Fold into triangle, point at top.
2. Turn lower edge up 1".
3. Turn over, folded edge down.
4. Roll tightly from left to right.
5. Tuck in corner. Stand upright.

Fan

Pretty in napkin ring or on plate.

Instructions:
1. Fold top and bottom edges to center.
2. Fold top and bottom edges to center a second time.
3. Pleat firmly from the left edge. Sharpen edges with hot iron.
4. Spread out fan. Balance flat folds of each side on table. Well-starched napkins will hold shape.

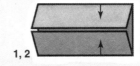

Lily

Effective and pretty on table.

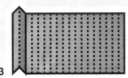

Instructions:
1. Fold napkin into quarters.
2. Fold into triangle, closed corner to open points.
3. Turn two points over to other side. (Two points are on either side of closed point.)
4. Pleat.
5. Place closed end in glass. Pull down two points on each side and shape.

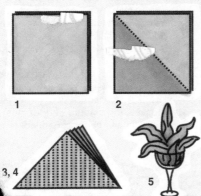

Measurements & Substitutions

Measurements

a pinch	1/8 teaspoon or less
3 teaspoons	1 tablespoon
4 tablespoons	1/4 cup
8 tablespoons	1/2 cup
12 tablespoons	3/4 cup
16 tablespoons	1 cup
2 cups	1 pint
4 cups	1 quart
4 quarts	1 gallon
8 quarts	1 peck
4 pecks	1 bushel
16 ounces	1 pound
32 ounces	1 quart
1 ounce liquid	2 tablespoons
8 ounces liquid	1 cup

**Use standard measuring spoons and cups.
All measurements are level.**

Substitutions

Ingredient	Quantity	Substitute
baking powder	1 teaspoon	1/4 tsp. baking soda plus 1/2 tsp. cream of tartar
catsup or chili sauce	1 cup	1 c. tomato sauce plus 1/2 c. sugar and 2 T. vinegar (for use in cooking)
chocolate	1 square (1 oz.)	3 or 4 T. cocoa plus 1 T. butter
cornstarch	1 tablespoon	2 T. flour or 2 tsp. quick-cooking tapioca
cracker crumbs	3/4 cup	1 c. bread crumbs
dates	1 lb.	1 1/2 c. dates, pitted and cut
dry mustard	1 teaspoon	1 T. prepared mustard
flour, self-rising	1 cup	1 c. all-purpose flour, 1/2 tsp. salt, and 1 tsp. baking powder
herbs, fresh	1 tablespoon	1 tsp. dried herbs
milk, sour	1 cup	1 T. lemon juice or vinegar plus sweet milk to make 1 c. (let stand 5 minutes)
whole	1 cup	1/2 c. evaporated milk plus 1/2 c. water
min. marshmallows	10	1 lg. marshmallow
onion, fresh	1 small	1 T. instant minced onion, rehydrated
sugar, brown	1/2 cup	2 T. molasses in 1/2 c. granulated sugar
powdered	1 cup	1 c. granulated sugar plus 1 tsp. cornstarch
tomato juice	1 cup	1/2 c. tomato sauce plus 1/2 c. water

**When substituting cocoa for chocolate in cakes, the amount of flour must
be reduced. Brown and white sugars usually can be interchanged.**

Equivalency Chart

Food	Quantity	Yield
apple	1 medium	1 cup
banana, mashed	1 medium	⅓ cup
bread	1 ½ slices	1 cup soft crumbs
bread	1 slice	¼ cup fine, dry crumbs
butter	1 stick or ¼ pound	½ cup
cheese, American, cubed	1 pound	2 ⅔ cups
American, grated	1 pound	5 cups
cream cheese	3-ounce package	6 ⅔ tablespoons
chocolate, bitter	1 square	1 ounce
cocoa	1 pound	4 cups
coconut	1 ½ pound package	2 ⅔ cups
coffee, ground	1 pound	5 cups
cornmeal	1 pound	3 cups
cornstarch	1 pound	3 cups
crackers, graham	14 squares	1 cup fine crumbs
saltine	28 crackers	1 cup fine crumbs
egg	4-5 whole	1 cup
whites	8-10	1 cup
yolks	10-12	1 cup
evaporated milk	1 cup	3 cups whipped
flour, cake, sifted	1 pound	4 ½ cups
rye	1 pound	5 cups
white, sifted	1 pound	4 cups
white, unsifted	1 pound	3 ¾ cups
gelatin, flavored	3 ¼ ounces	½ cup
unflavored	¼ ounce	1 tablespoon
lemon	1 medium	3 tablespoon juice
marshmallows	16	¼ pound
noodles, cooked	8-ounce package	7 cups
uncooked	4 ounces (1 ½ cups)	2-3 cups cooked
macaroni, cooked	8-ounce package	6 cups
macaroni, uncooked	4 ounces (1 ¼ cups)	2 ¼ cups cooked
spaghetti, uncooked	7 ounces	4 cups cooked
nuts, chopped	¼ pound	1 cup
almonds	1 pound	3 ½ cups
walnuts, broken	1 pound	3 cups
walnuts, unshelled	1 pound	1 ½ to 1 ¾ cups
onion	1 medium	½ cup
orange	3-4 medium	1 cup juice
raisins	1 pound	3 ½ cups
rice, brown	1 cup	4 cups cooked
converted	1 cup	3 ½ cups cooked
regular	1 cup	3 cups cooked
wild	1 cup	4 cups cooked
sugar, brown	1 pound	2 ½ cups
powdered	1 pound	3 ½ cups
white	1 pound	2 cups
vanilla wafers	22	1 cup fine crumbs
zwieback, crumbled	4	1 cups

Food Quantities
For Large Servings

	25 Servings	50 Servings	100 Servings
Beverages:			
coffee	½ pound and 1 ½ gallons water	1 pound and 3 gallons water	2 pounds and 6 gallons water
lemonade	10-15 lemons and 1 ½ gallons water	20-30 lemons and 3 gallons water	40-60 lemons and 6 gallons water
tea	1/12 pound and 1 ½ gallons water	⅙ pound and 3 gallons water	⅓ pound and 6 gallons water
Desserts:			
layered cake	1 12" cake	3 10" cakes	6 10" cakes
sheet cake	1 10" x 12" cake	1 12" x 20" cake	2 12" x 20" cakes
watermelon	37 ½ pounds	75 pounds	150 pounds
whipping cream	¾ pint	1 ½ to 2 pints	3-4 pints
Ice cream:			
brick	3 ¼ quarts	6 ½ quarts	13 quarts
bulk	2 ¼ quarts	4 ½ quarts or 1 ¼ gallons	9 quarts or 2 ½ gallons
Meat, poultry or fish:			
fish	13 pounds	25 pounds	50 pounds
fish, fillets or steak	7 ½ pounds	15 pounds	30 pounds
hamburger	9 pounds	18 pounds	35 pounds
turkey or chicken	13 pounds	25 to 35 pounds	50 to 75 pounds
wieners (beef)	6 ½ pounds	13 pounds	25 pounds
Salads, casseroles:			
baked beans	¾ gallon	1 ¼ gallons	2 ½ gallons
jello salad	¾ gallon	1 ¼ gallons	2 ½ gallons
potato salad	4 ¼ quarts	2 ¼ gallons	4 ½ gallons
scalloped potatoes	4 ½ quarts or 1 12" x 20" pan	9 quarts or 2 ¼ gallons	18 quarts 4 ½ gallons
spaghetti	1 ¼ gallons	2 ½ gallons	5 gallons
Sandwiches:			
bread	50 slices or 3 1-pound loaves	100 slices or 6 1-pound loaves	200 slices or 12 1-pound loaves
butter	½ pound	1 pound	2 pounds
lettuce	1 ½ heads	3 heads	6 heads
mayonnaise	1 cup	2 cups	4 cups
mixed filling			
meat, eggs, fish	1 ½ quarts	3 quarts	6 quarts
jam, jelly	1 quart	2 quarts	4 quarts

Microwave Hints

1. Place an open box of hardened brown sugar in the microwave oven with 1 cup hot water. Microwave on high for 1 1/2 to 2 minutes for 1/2 pound or 2 to 3 minutes for 1 pound.

2. Soften hard ice cream by microwaving at 30% power. One pint will take 15 to 30 seconds; one quart, 30-45 seconds; and one-half gallon, 45-60 seconds.

3. To melt chocolate, place 1/2 pound in glass bowl or measuring cup. Melt uncovered at 50% power for 3-4 minutes; stir after 2 minutes.

4. Soften one 8-ounce package of cream cheese by microwaving at 30% power for 2 to 2 1/2 minutes. One 3-ounce package of cream cheese will soften in 1 1/2 to 2 minutes.

5. A 4 1/2 ounce carton of whipped topping will thaw in 1 minute on the defrost setting. Whipped topping should be slightly firm in the center, but it will blend well when stirred. Do not over thaw!

6. Soften jello that has set up too hard - perhaps you were to chill it until slightly thickened and forgot it. Heat on a low power setting for a very short time.

7. Heat hot packs. A wet fingertip towel will take about 25 seconds. It depends on the temperature of the water used to wet the towel.

8. To scald milk, cook 1 cup for 2 to 2 1/2 minutes, stirring once each minute.

9. To make dry bread crumbs, cut 6 slices of bread into 1/2-inch cubes. Microwave in 3-quart casserole 6-7 minutes, or until dry, stirring after 3 minutes. Crush in blender.

10. Refresh stale potato chips, crackers or other snacks of such type by putting a plateful in the microwave for 30-45 seconds. Let stand for 1 minute to crisp. Cereals can also be crisped.

11. Nuts will be easier to shell if you place 2 cups of nuts in a 1-quart casserole with 1 cup of water. Cook for 4 to 5 minutes and the nutmeats will slip out whole after cracking the shell.

12. Stamp collectors can place a few drops of water on a stamp to remove it from an envelope. Heat in the microwave for 20 seconds, and the stamp will come off.

13. Using a round dish instead of a square one eliminates overcooked corners in baking cakes.

14. Sprinkle a layer of medium, finely chopped walnuts evenly onto the bottom and side of a ring pan or bundt cake pan to enhances the looks and eating quality. Pour in batter and microwave as recipe directs.

15. Do not salt foods on the surface as it causes dehydration and toughens food. Salt after you remove from the oven unless the recipe calls for using salt in the mixture.

16. Heat left-over custard and use it as frosting for a cake.

17. Melt marshmallow cream. Half of a 7-ounce jar will melt in 35-40 seconds on high. Stir to blend.

18. To toast coconut, spread 1/2 cup coconut in a pie plate and cook for 3-4 minutes, stirring every 30 seconds after 2 minutes. Watch closely, as it quickly browns.

19. To melt crystallized honey, heat uncovered jar on high for 30-45 seconds. If jar is large, repeat.

20. One stick of butter or margarine will soften in 1 minute when microwaved at 20% power.

Calorie Counter

Beverages

apple juice, 6 oz. 90
coffee (black) 0
cola type, 12 oz. 115
cranberry juice, 6 oz. 115
ginger ale, 12 oz. 115
grape juice, (prepared from
   frozen concentrate), 6 oz. 142
lemonade, (prepared from
   frozen concentrate), 6 oz. 85
milk, protein fortified, 1 c...................105
   skim, 1 c. 90
   whole, 1 c. 160
orange juice, 6 oz. 85
pineapple juice, unsweetened, 6 oz.......95
root beer, 12 oz. 150
tonic (quinine water) 12 oz. 132

Breads

cornbread, 1 sm. square 130
dumplings, 1 med. 70
French toast, 1 slice 135
melba toast, 1 slice 25
muffins, blueberry, 1 muffin 110
   bran, 1 muffin..............................106
   corn, 1 muffin..............................125
   English, 1 muffin 280
pancakes, 1 (4-in.) 60
pumpernickel, 1 slice 75
rye, 1 slice 60
waffle, 1 216
white, 1 slice 60-70
whole wheat, 1 slice 55-65

Cereals

cornflakes, 1 c....................................105
cream of wheat, 1 c. 120
oatmeal, 1 c. 148
rice flakes, 1 c. 105
shredded wheat, 1 biscuit 100
sugar krisps, 3/4 c. 110

Crackers

graham, 1 cracker 15-30
rye crisp, 1 cracker.............................35
saltine, 1 cracker...........................17-20
wheat thins, 1 cracker 9

Dairy Products

butter or margarine, 1 T....................100
cheese, American, 1 oz. 100
   camembert, 1 oz. 85
   cheddar, 1 oz. 115
   cottage cheese, 1 oz. 30
   mozzarella, 1 oz. 90
   parmesan, 1 oz. 130
   ricotta, 1 oz...................................50
   roquefort, 1 oz. 105
   Swiss, 1 oz. 105
cream, light, 1 T. 30
   heavy, 1 T. 55
   sour, 1 T. 45
hot chocolate, with milk, 1 c. 277
milk chocolate, 1 oz. 145-155
yogurt
   made w/ whole milk, 1 c. 150-165
   made w/ skimmed milk, 1 c. 125

Eggs

fried, 1 lg. 100
poached or boiled, 1 lg. 75-80
scrambled or in omelet, 1 lg. 110-130

Fish and Seafood

bass, 4 oz. 105
salmon, broiled or baked, 3 oz. 155
sardines, canned in oil, 3 oz. 170
trout, fried, 3 1/2 oz. 220
tuna, in oil, 3 oz. 170
   in water, 3 oz. 110

Calorie Counter

Fruits

apple, 1 med. 80-100
applesauce, sweetened, 1/2 c. 90-115
    unsweetened, 1/2 c............................50
banana, 1 med. 85
blueberries, 1/2 c.................................45
cantaloupe, 1/2 c.................................24
cherries (pitted), raw, 1/2 c. 40
grapefruit, 1/2 med. 55
grapes, 1/2 c. 35-55
honeydew, 1/2 c. 55
mango, 1 med. 90
orange, 1 med. 65-75
peach, 1 med. 35
pear, 1 med. 60-100
pineapple, fresh, 1/2 c...........................40
    canned in syrup, 1/2 c. 95
plum, 1 med. 30
strawberries, fresh, 1/2 c.......................30
    frozen and sweetened, 1/2 c. 120-140
tangerine, 1 lg. 39
watermelon, 1/2 c. 42

Meat and Poultry

beef, ground (lean), 3 oz. 185
    roast, 3 oz. 185
chicken, broiled, 3 oz..........................115
lamb chop (lean), 3 oz. 175-200
steak, sirloin, 3 oz. 175
    tenderloin, 3 oz. 174
    top round, 3 oz. 162
turkey, dark meat, 3 oz. 175
    white meat, 3 oz. 150
veal, cutlet, 3 oz................................156
    roast, 3 oz. 76

Nuts

almonds, 2 T. 105
cashews, 2 T. 100
peanuts, 2 T. 105
peanut butter, 1 T. 95
pecans, 2 T. 95
pistachios, 2 T. 92
walnuts, 2 T. 80

Pasta

macaroni or spaghetti,
    cooked, 3/4 c. 115

Salad Dressings

blue cheese, 1 T....................................70
French, 1 T...65
Italian, 1 T. 80
mayonnaise, 1 T...................................100
olive oil, 1 T. 124
Russian, 1 T..70
salad oil, 1 T.......................................120

Soups

bean, 1 c. 130-180
beef noodle, 1 c....................................70
bouillon and consomme, 1 c. 30
chicken noodle, 1 c. 65
chicken with rice, 1 c. 50
minestrone, 1 c.............................80-150
split pea, 1 c. 145-170
tomato with milk, 1 c. 170
vegetable, 1 c. 80-100

Vegetables

asparagus, 1 c. 35
broccoli, cooked, 1/2 c. 25
cabbage, cooked, 1/2 c. 15-20
carrots, cooked, 1/2 c. 25-30
cauliflower, 1/2 c. 10-15
corn (kernels), 1/2 c. 70
green beans, 1 c. 30
lettuce, shredded, 1/2 c..........................5
mushrooms, canned, 1/2 c. 20
onions, cooked, 1/2 c. 30
peas, cooked, 1/2 c...............................60
potato, baked, 1 med. 90
    chips, 8-10 100
    mashed, w/milk & butter, 1 c. ..200-300
spinach, 1 c. 40
tomato, raw, 1 med. 25
    cooked, 1/2 c. 30

Cooking Terms

Au gratin: Topped with crumbs and/or cheese and browned in oven or under broiler.

Au jus: Served in its own juices.

Baste: To moisten foods during cooking with pan drippings or special sauce in order to add flavor and prevent drying.

Bisque: A thick cream soup.

Blanch: To immerse in rapidly boiling water and allow to cook slightly.

Cream: To soften a fat, especially butter, by beating it at room temperature. Butter and sugar are often creamed together, making a smooth, soft paste.

Crimp: To seal the edges of a two-crust pie either by pinching them at intervals with the fingers or by pressing them together with the tines of a fork.

Crudites: An assortment of raw vegetables (i.e. carrots, broccoli, celery, mushrooms) that is served as an hors d'oeuvre, often accompanied by a dip.

Degrease: To remove fat from the surface of stews, soups, or stock. Usually cooled in the refrigerator so that fat hardens and is easily removed.

Dredge: To coat lightly with flour, corn-meal, etc.

Entree: The main course.

Fold: To incorporate a delicate substance, such as whipped cream or beaten egg whites, into another substance without releasing air bubbles. A spatula is used to gently bring part of the mixture from the bottom of the bowl to the top. The process is repeated, while slowly rotating the bowl, until the ingredients are thoroughly blended.

Glaze: To cover with a glossy coating, such as a melted and somewhat diluted jelly for fruit desserts.

Julienne: To cut vegetables, fruits, or cheeses into match-shaped slivers.

Marinate: To allow food to stand in a liquid in order to tenderize or to add flavor.

Meuniére: Dredged with flour and sautéed in butter.

Mince: To chop food into very small pieces.

Parboil: To boil until partially cooked; to blanch. Usually final cooking in a seasoned sauce follows this procedure.

Pare: To remove the outermost skin of a fruit or vegetable.

Poach: To cook gently in hot liquid kept just below the boiling point.

Purée: To mash foods by hand by rubbing through a sieve or food mill, or by whirling in a blender or food processor until perfectly smooth.

Refresh: To run cold water over food that has been parboiled in order to stop the cooking process quickly.

Sauté: To cook and/or brown food in a small quantity of hot shortening.

Scald: To heat to just below the boiling point, when tiny bubbles appear at the edge of the saucepan.

Simmer: To cook in liquid just below the boiling point. The surface of the liquid should be barely moving, broken from time to time by slowly rising bubbles.

Steep: To let food stand in hot liquid in order to extract or to enhance flavor, like tea in hot water or poached fruit in sugar syrup.

Toss: To combine ingredients with a repeated lifting motion.

Whip: To beat rapidly in order to incorporate air and produce expansion, as in heavy cream or egg whites.